HORRIBLE HISTORIES

VILE VICTORIANS

Terry Deary
Illustrated by **Martin Brown**

■SCHOLASTIC

Scholastic Children's Books,
Euston House, 24 Eversholt Street,
London, NW1 1DB, UK

A division of Scholastic Ltd
London ~ New York ~ Toronto ~ Sydney ~ Auckland
Mexico City ~ New Delhi ~ Hong Kong

First published in the UK by Scholastic Ltd, 1994
This edition published 2007

Some of the material in this book has previously been published in Horrible Histories
The Massive Millennium Quiz Book/Horrible Huge Quiz Book

Text copyright © Terry Deary, 1994, 1999
Illustrations © Martin Brown, 1994, 1999
All rights reserved

10 digit ISBN 0 439 94404 X
13 digit ISBN 978 0439 94404 5

Printed in the UK by CPI Bookmarque, Croydon

20 19 18 17 16 15 14 13 12 11

The right of Terry Deary and Martin Brown to be identified as the author and illustrators of this work respectively has been asserted by them in accordance with the Copyright, Designs and Patents Act, 1988.

This book is sold subject to the condition that it shall not, by way of trade or otherwise be lent, resold, hired out, or otherwise circulated without the publisher's prior consent in any form of binding or cover other than that in which it is published and without a similar condition, including this condition, being imposed on a subsequent purchaser.

Contents

Introduction 5

Vile Victorian timelines 7

Vile Victorian Queen 12

Vile Victorian childhood 22

Vile Victorian schools 44

Vile Victorian fun and games 54

Vile Victorian poems, plays and songs 64

Vile Victorian life 73

Vile Victorian food 90

Vile Victorian facts 94

The vile Victorian Army 99

Vile Victorian villains 112

Epilogue 128

Grisly Quiz 129

Interesting Index 137

Introduction

History can be horrible! Sometimes you can have horribly clever teachers using horribly funny words...

> THE VICTORIANS WERE VILE WHAT'S VILE, SARAH?
>
> PLEASE, SIR, A VILE'S WHAT I CLEAN MY VINGERNAILS WITH!
>
> STUPID CHILD!

But you may find that history can be horribly exciting. Stories of great and gory deeds. Even a teacher can get carried away by stirring tales of daring deeds performed by our ancestors...

> INTO THE VALLEY OF DEATH RODE THE SIX HUNDRED!
>
> I THINK HE'S GETTING CARRIED AWAY!

And sometimes history can be horribly horrible. Some of the things that happened to people may seem horribly disgusting to us...

> ...AND THE CHOLERA VICTIMS TURNED BLUE BEFORE THEY DIED
>
> PLEASE, SIR, FIONA'S JUST TURNED GREEN, WHAT'S SHE GOT?

That's the sort of history you'll find here. Be warned! This book is not for the squeamish. If you have a weak stomach then don't read it – or, if you have to read it, then read it with your eyes closed.

You wouldn't believe some of the things the vile Victorians got up to. After you've read this book you still might not believe them. But they are true, I'm afraid. Some Victorians could be Vicious and Violent and Villainous – Vile, in fact.

When you've finished the book you'll probably know more fascinating facts about the Victorians than your teacher. You may find that History is absolutely Horrible – but learning about it is horribly fascinating.

Be warned, again! This book is not suitable for adults. Victorian adults did some pretty nasty things to children. You wouldn't want your parents or teachers to get any horrible ideas, would you?

Vile Victorian timelines

The good

1837 Victoria becomes queen at the age of 18.

1838 Northumberland girl, Grace Darling, rescues five survivors of a shipwreck.

1830s William Henry Fox Talbot prints his first photographs.

1840 World's first sticky postage stamp – the Penny Black – goes on sale.

1842 Law passed to ban women and children from working in mines.

1851 The Great Exhibition (of British industry) opens in the Crystal Palace.

1852 The first men's flushing public toilet opens in London – that's a relief!

1867 Joseph Lister, surgeon, uses a disinfectant, Phenol; deaths after surgery fall from 45 per cent to just 15 per cent.

1868 Wilkie Collins writes the first 'detective' story, *The Moonstone*.

1871 Queen Vic opens the Albert Hall, named after her husband – Albert, that is, not Hall!

1877 Mr Boot opens a chemist's shop . . . and another. (So we have the first pair of Boots).

1883 First electric railway – a shocking success.

1887 First Sherlock Holmes story published – the case called *A Study in Scarlet*.

1896 First moving pictures seen in public in Britain – films including *The Boxing Kangaroo*, *Three Skirt Dancers* and *The Epsom Derby* were shown in London.

1901 A non-league club wins the FA Cup. They call themselves Tottenham Hotspur.

The bad

1842 A report reveals that half of all children die before their fifth birthday.

1845 Famine in Ireland as the potato crop fails.

1851 The first cigarettes are sold in Britain – people have been dying for a smoke ever since.

1853 Small earthquake shakes the south of the country.

1854 British troops fight Russian in the Crimea – Florrie Nightingale patches them up.

1858 Telegraph cable laid from Britain to America – it snaps 28 days later!

1861 Prince Albert dies. Victoria goes into mourning . . . and stays there for the rest of her life!

1870 Charles Dickens dies, 'exhausted by fame' – but filthy rich.

1882 England Cricketers lose to Australia at the Oval for the first time! National disaster! British pride burnt to Ashes!

1883 *Treasure Island* written by Stevenson. 'A story for boys – women are excluded', he says. Typical.

1890 The first comic, *Comic Cuts*, is printed. As a man dodges a dart he cries, 'That was an arrow escape!' (Groan!).

1891 Education **FREE** for every child – now there's **no** excuse for not going to school.

1896 Speed Limit for cars increased 400 per cent – from 4 mph to 20 mph! Men with red flags out of a job!

1897 George Smith, London Taxi driver, is the first drunken driver ever.

1901 Queen Vic dies aged 81.

The ugly

1837 Robert Cocking jumps 180 metres from a balloon to test a parachute. It doesn't work. Splatt!

1846 Report says over 40,000 people are living in cramped cellars in Liverpool.

1849 Two thousand people a week die in the latest cholera epidemic – they get rotten diarrhoea, turn blue and then die.

1854 The last of London's great medieval fairs, Bartholomew Fair, is banned. People enjoy it too much!

1857 Indian rebels massacre bullying British rulers in India so British soldiers massacre Indians.

1870 An Education Act means school for everyone . . . and that means **YOU** . . . but it costs a penny a day.

1872 The empty ship, *Mary Celeste*, found adrift in the Atlantic – did the crew meet a gruesome end?

1879 The British army takes on the Zulus at Isandhlwana – the Zulus 'washed their spears' in British blood. Yeuch!

1883 Matthew Webb, who swam the English Channel in 1875, dies trying to swim rapids above Niagara Falls. Not a good idea.

1888 Jack the Ripper strikes in London – he is never caught.

1894 Blackpool Tower opens – a copy of the Eiffel Tower in Paris.

1897 Nine-year-old boy crushed by London taxi. First ever road death ... of many.

1899 Percy Pilcher (honest, that's his name) flies in a hang glider – but not for long. Lands on head. Splatt. Dead.

Vile Victorian Queen

Victoria lost her father when she was eight months old. She lost her husband, Albert, when she was 42. The only thing she couldn't lose was her sense of humour . . . she never had one! Here are . . .

Ten things you should know about Victoria

1   Victoria's father was Edward Duke of Kent, the fourth son of George III. The playwright, Sheridan, suggested that Edward was bald because he hadn't enough brains inside his head to feed hair on the outside. What he actually said was, 'Grass does not grow upon deserts'.

2   She discovered she was heir to the throne when she was nearly eleven years old. She immediately promised, 'I will be good!' She meant, 'I will be a good little teacher's pet from now on.' Later, people twisted the meaning of these words and said she meant, 'I will be a good queen when I get my fat little bottom on the throne.'

3   Victoria could hardly wait. When the Lord Chamberlain brought her the news of William IV's death he ended by saying ' . . . you are the Queen.' No sooner had he got the word 'Queen' out of his mouth than Victoria shot out a hand for him to kiss.

4 The Queen did not grow to five feet tall – she made up for it by being about five feet wide in later life. Funnily enough this 'shortest' British monarch ruled 'longest' of any of them.

5 Victoria fell in love with her cousin Albert at first sight. She wrote ... *Albert is really quite charming, and so excessively handsome, such beautiful blue eyes, an exquisite nose, and such a pretty mouth with delicate moustachios and slight but very slight whiskers; a beautiful figure, broad in the shoulders and a fine waist.* Soon after, Victoria proposed to Albert.

6 Albert died in 1861. A historian, Lytton Strachey, described Victoria's agony at Albert's death ... *She shrieked – one long wild shriek that ran through the horror-stricken castle – and understood that she had lost him forever.* She became a changed woman. She refused for many years to appear in public. Then, when she did, she insisted on wearing her black widow's bonnet and not a crown.

7 Victoria spent much of her time in Scotland where she had a devoted manservant, John Brown. Rumours said that Brown had married Victoria (not true), that Victoria stopped him from marrying one of her maids (probably true) and that he was a 'Spiritualist' – he held seances in the room where Albert died and let Victoria talk to her dead husband (almost certainly not true!). He died in 1883.

8 The Queen's favourite Prime Minister was Benjamin Disraeli. In 1876 he had the Royal Titles Bill passed which made her Empress. (She was the first, last and only British Empress of India). As Disraeli lay dying in 1881, someone suggested that the Queen should come and visit him. He replied. "She would only ask me to take a message to Albert.'

'BETTER NOT, SHE WOULD ONLY ASK ME TO TAKE A MESSAGE TO ALBERT'

9 Victoria's least favourite Prime Minister was William Gladstone. She said he was 'half crazy and, really in many ways, a ridiculous old man.' The admiring public nicknamed him G.O.M. – Grand Old Man. Disraeli said it stood for God's Only Mistake!

10 Queen Vic survived seven attempts to assassinate her. The first three attempts took place in 1842. As the Queen rode in London's Mall with Albert, a man came out of the crowd and fired a pistol at her. He was just six or seven paces away. The gun misfired!

You would think Victoria would have learned her lesson. The very next day Victoria rode past the same spot ... and the same man fired again! The gun only had a blank in it, but John Francis, the gunman, was still sentenced to death. He was granted a reprieve before he was executed.

> LINE UP! LINE UP! HAVE A POT AT THE QUEEN, THREE SHOTS A PENNY!

In July of that same year, a youth with a pathetic face fired at Queen Victoria as she was out riding in her carriage. Luckily for Queen Vic, the youth, John Bean, had put more paper and tobacco in the pistol than gunpowder.

Ten useless bits of information about Victoria...

1 Victoria had bishopophobia – a fear of bishops. When she was a little girl she was scared of their wigs. Her dislike of bishops lasted all her life.

2 As a child she could be a bad-tempered little madam. Her music teacher told her she 'must' practice the piano if she wanted to learn. She slammed the piano lid and snapped,

'THERE! YOU SEE, THERE IS NO "MUST" ABOUT IT!'

When she was playing with a friend she once said...

'YOU MUST NOT TOUCH THOSE TOYS, THEY ARE MINE, AND I MAY CALL YOU JANE, BUT YOU MUST NOT CALL ME VICTORIA'

3 Victoria's coronation was quite an event, with the lords of the land queuing up to touch her crown as part of the ceremony. Some couldn't quite manage the last four steps up to the throne, as Harriet Martineau described . . .

Lord Rolle, a large and feeble old man, had to be held up by two lords. He had nearly reached the royal footstool when he slipped through the hands of the two lords and rolled over and over down the steps, lying at the bottom coiled up in his robes. He was instantly lifted up and he tried again and again amid shouts of admiration for his bravery. It turned me very sick.

One unkind witness suggested that he got the title of Lord 'Rolle' because of his coronation trick!

The ladies were as gruesome as the old lord. Harriet described them as . . .
Old hags, with their dyed or false hair drawn to the top of the head to allow them to put on their coronets. They had their necks and arms bare and glittering with diamonds; and those necks were so brown and wrinkled as to make one sick; or dusted over with white powder which was worse than what it disguised.

4 The coronation was curious in other ways. The Archbishop placed the coronation ring on the wrong finger and Victoria suffered 'great pain' in getting it off again. She went into a chapel at the side of the abbey where the Archbishop was supposed to give her the golden Orb. He couldn't. Victoria already had it!

The Queen's Treasurer scattered gold and silver medals among the lordly congregation . . . but that caused a lot of 'turbulent scrimmaging' as they fought to pick them up! It was reported that . . .
The Aldermen of London sprawled over the floor in their furred gowns and grabbed one another by the sleeves in their rude scramble for the pieces.

tinkle tinkle

5 Victoria's weight caused her adviser, Lord Melbourne, to nag her...

> YOU SHOULD DO MORE WALKING
>
> WHEN I WALK I GET STONES IN MY SHOES

> THEN HAVE YOUR SHOES MADE TIGHTER. PRINCESS CHARLOTTE DIED OF NOT WALKING
>
> MY FEET SWELL

> DO MORE THEN!
>
> NO!

> YES!
>
> THE QUEEN OF SPAIN IS EVER SO FAT AND SHE DOES LOTS OF WALKING

Lord Melbourne had no answer to that. Victoria didn't take up exercise. She got fat instead. The royal doctor said, 'She is more like a barrel than anything else.'

6 Queen Victoria's son-in-law, Prince Christian, was a truly vile Victorian. He lost an eye in a shooting accident. At dinner parties he would have a footman deliver his collection of glass eyes to the table. Christian would then tell the story of each eye. His favourite was the bloodshot one which he wore when he had a cold!

7 Victoria's most famous 'saying' is, 'We are not amused.' Her diaries are full of the phrase, 'I was very much amused,' but she never, ever said or wrote, 'We are not amused.' It's just a story! So there, now you know.

8 Old Victoria died in January 1901. She was buried with a picture of John Brown and a lock of his hair wrapped in tissue. The dead Queen's hair was cut off to be put into lockets for friends and family.

9 Victoria's vile son Edward became King Edward VII when she died. He was particularly fond of hunting. He once chased a deer from Harrow to Paddington where it was cornered at Paddington Station and killed as railway porters and guards watched. He shot down an elephant in Africa, hacked off its tail and jumped on its side to do a dance. But the elephant was only stunned, not dead. It rose to its feet and staggered off into the jungle... not wagging its tail! Edward wrote a letter home, complaining that the leeches in Africa 'climb up your legs and bight you.' He was even worse at spelling than he was at shooting elephants!

> IT WAS REALLY ODD.... WHEN I WOKE UP I WAS BEING DANCED ON BY THIS FAT ENGLISH BLOKE AND MY TAIL WAS GONE

10 Victoria lived so long that Edward was an old man before he came to the throne. He complained...
I don't mind praying to the Eternal Father, but I must be the only man in the country plagued with an eternal mother.

Vile Victorian childhood

Vile Victorian parents – or, growing up is hard to do!

You may think your parents are pretty vile. They nag you to tidy your room, force you to eat your spinach and wear sensible clothes.

But at least you have some room, some food and some clothes! Many Victorian children weren't that lucky! When a new Victorian baby arrived, people would ask, 'Has it come to stay?' Growing up for many was like getting over an obstacle course of death.

MEET TINY TIM® THE NINETEENTH CENTURY ACTION BABY – THE VICTORIAN TOT WITH A LOAD OF SURVIVING TO DO!

1 An 1860s report said . . .
In the last five years, in this district alone, at least 278 infants were murdered; more than 60 were found dead in the Thames or the canals or ponds of London and many more than a hundred were found dead, under railway arches, on doorsteps, in dustholes, cellars and the like.

And those were just the ones the police **knew** about. Many more babies suffocated at birth and the doctors didn't notice the cloth, dough or mud that had been used to smother them – 'Death by natural causes,' they said.

2 Let's face it – babies are smelly, noisy and expensive to keep. Some parents decided that the best way to deal with this was to send their child to a 'Baby Farm' – no that's not a nice place in the country like a sheep farm! A baby-farmer was a woman who would offer to look after your children for you. For five pounds you need never see your child again. Of course, the baby-farmer couldn't raise a child for life on five pounds, so the babies were neglected. If the baby died then that saved money. Baby-farmer, Margaret Walters, was brought to trial for her treatment of baby Cowan, who was described as . . .

scarcely a bit of flesh on the bones. It could only be recognised by the hair. It did not cry, being much too weak for that. It was scarcely human; I mean that it looked more like a monkey than a child. It was a shadow.

Baby Cowan died. Baby-farmer Walters was hanged.

3 You may object to sharing a bedroom with a grotty little brother. But in the 1860s, James Greenwood saw . . .

. . . grown persons sleeping with their parents, brothers and sisters, occupying the same bed of filthy rags or straw. I have note of a locality where 48 men, 73 women and 59 children are living in 34 rooms. In one house I found a single room with one man, two women and two children; and there was the dead body of a poor girl who had died a few days before. The body was stretched out on the bare floor without a shroud or coffin.

A French visitor, Hippolyte Taine, found a London family 'whose only bed was a heap of soot; they had been sleeping on it for some months.'

4 There wasn't enough food around to fatten a scavenging cat. Hippolyte said he saw . . .
A miserable black cat, skinny, limping, half stupefied. It was watching an old woman fearfully out of one eye while sniffing and pawing through a pile of rubbish. No doubt it was right to be nervous – the old woman was watching it with a look as hungry as its own, and mumbling. It looked to me as if she were thinking there went two pounds of meat.

5 As soon as a child could crawl it could work. Making matchboxes was a boring, badly paid job, but at least children could do it from a very early age. If that was too boring then you could go on the street corners and sell the matches. You might not be able to afford shoes so you would freeze to death.

6 The young Doctor Barnardo from Dublin wanted to be a medical missionary in China. When he saw the state of the London children he decided he was more needed there. He opened homes for orphan children and educated them too. Many went to good jobs in England and abroad. Most of the girls went into service at the age of 16.

You've survived!

Getting a good job as a servant is proof that you've survived the Growing-up Game of life and death in London . . . But would you get that job? When you left Barnardo's you were placed in a division. Here are the four 'Divisions' you could be placed in at the age of 13 . . . Which one would **YOU** end up in?

First Division:

All girls who, at 16, have a good record of conduct and character. They will receive an outfit worth five pounds which they can keep if they stay in their first job 12 months. If they have a good report after 12 months they will receive a special prize.

Second Division:

Girls who have frequently given way to ill temper, disobedience, insolence, laziness or other grave faults cannot be placed in the first division, but if they make a special effort in their final year to improve then they may be placed in the second division. They will receive an outfit worth three pounds and ten shillings and if they have a good report after 12 months will also receive a prize.

Third Division:
Girls who up to the time of their leaving continue to show bad conduct, ill temper, self-will, disobedience or insolence can only be placed in the third division with their mistress being informed of their faults. They will receive a third class outfit, value three pounds, the whole of which must be paid for out of their own wages. A girl in the third division will not be eligible for a prize till she has been in service two years and has earned a good report.

Fourth Division:
Girls who are found to be dishonest, regularly untruthful, violent and uncontrolled in temper, vicious, or unclean in their personal habits, will not be sent out to service, nor will they have an outfit but will be dismissed from Barnardo's in disgrace or sent to a school of discipline.

So? Where would **YOU** end up? And if you ended up in the first division would you **WANT** to be a maidservant in Victorian London? Here is a typical day.

A day in the life of a parlour maid – or, is it worth going to bed?

Morning tasks

6.00 Get out of bed, wash, dress, brush hair into a bun.

6.30 Go downstairs. Put the kettle on. Pull up blinds, open windows, clean fireplaces.

7.00 Make early tea and take it to master and mistress.

7.30 Sweep the dining room and dust. Lay the table for breakfast.

8.00 Serve breakfast.

8.30 Go upstairs, strip the beds, open the bedroom windows, have own breakfast.

9.00 Clear breakfast table, wash up, put on clean apron, make the beds, clean the taps, wash the baths and bathroom floors, clean the toilets, dust every bedroom.

12.00 Change dress to serve lunch; lay the lunch table, serve the lunch, clear the table, wash up all the glass and silver, put everything away in its place.

1.00 Clean the pantry sink and floor, eat own lunch.

Afternoon tasks

ᘓDAILY GRIND REMINDERᘔ
2·00 pm – 6·00 pm

Monday: Help with laundry, wash brushes and combs, clear out pantry
Make sure to get the grease off the master's comb!

Tuesday: Clear out dining room, clean windows, clean fireplaces
after fireplace WASH HANDS before cleaning windows

Wednesday: Clear out a bedroom and a dressing room
Mistress's bedroom; keep the cat out

Thursday: Clean all the silver cutlery, plates and ornaments
Polish the Master's domino trophies v. carefully

Friday: Clean toilets, passage, stairs and hall
don't forget the fiddly bits

Saturday: Clean out servants' bedrooms
do Cook's first OR ELSE!!!
Cook

Sunday: Afternoon off
(sleep)

Evening tasks

6.00 Lay the table for dinner.

7.00 Serve dinner and wait at table.

8.30 Clear dinner table, wash up.

10.00 Eat own supper, wash up.

10.30 Go to bed.

Next day... start all over again. Of course, you would be paid. Paid nearly six pounds – six pounds a **YEAR** that is! And that's what you'd get for being a **GOOD** girl!

Five rules for servants

1 **No followers** – that is to say, no boyfriends for the maidservants. The mistress of the house didn't want strange men hanging around and she didn't want anyone getting married so she lost their services just as she had got them fully trained.

2 **No dishonesty** – a common trick was for the mistress to hide a coin under a carpet. If the servant didn't find the coin then she hadn't done the sweeping properly – she'd be sacked; if she **did** find the coin and kept it then, of course, she'd be sacked for dishonesty!

DON'T OVER-DO IT DEAR!

3 **Wear a uniform** – men had to wear dark suits or evening dress; women had to buy (or make) a cotton dress for morning wear and a black wool dress with a white cap and apron for the afternoons. (As a special treat she might be given some cloth as a Christmas present to make a new dress!)

4 **Stay invisible** – servants were to keep out of the way as much as possible; if a lady or gentleman of the house appeared, they had to stand aside to let them pass.

5 **Stay fit** – a sick servant cost money to keep fed and housed. The ill or the very old would usually be dismissed to make room for a fitter or younger person.

So, life as a servant could be hard and the hours long. But at least the work wasn't usually **dangerous**. Life in the coal mines, on the other hand, could be positively deadly – even for children . . .

The Monster of the mine

I

'Deep below the ground there's a great dark monster,' Granny Milburn mumbled through her toothless mouth.

'What does it look like?' Geordie asked.

'No one knows. They never see it, only hear its rattling roar and then its iron claws strike sparks from off the railway lines!' the old woman said and scrubbed her grandson's skinny back as he shivered in the old tin bath.

'And what does this dark monster do?'

'It eats up little boys that fall asleep below the ground,' she warned.

'But just the ones that fall asleep?'

'Yes. Just the ones that fall asleep!'

'But is this story true, Gran?' little Geordie breathed and his big grey eyes glinted fearful in the firelight.

The woman helped her grandson from the bath and rubbed him with a dry cloth. 'You had a brother, Tommy, once. He was just your age – just eight years old. One day he went off down the mine. He never came back home.'

'What happened, Gran? The monster? Did it get him?' young Geordie cried, and shuddered in his nightshirt.

'What's all this talk of monsters?' Geordie's mam asked as she came into the room. Her arms were full of cold, wet washing which she spread on some wooden rails above the fire to dry.

'Our Granny says there's monsters down the mine,' the boy said.

'Don't listen to your Gran!' his mam said wearily. 'You're eight years old – too old for fairy tales . . . we need the money that you'll get down Burnhope pit. Ten pence every week while your poor dad's laid off with coal dust in his chest.'

'I know, mam . . . and I want to work. It's just I'm scared the monster's going to get me!'

'Now get to bed!' his mother snapped and pushed him to the door. 'And don't you wake your father up or else he'll take his belt to you!'

'I won't, mam! Night Gran!'

'Good night, boy!' Granny Milburn sighed, then muttered, 'God preserve you down that mine.'

Geordie took a candle and stepped around his dad who snored upon some straw-sacks on the floor. The boy slipped between his three young sisters and his baby brother. His mother wrapped a blanket round his body and whispered, 'I'll wake you up at three o'clock tomorrow morning. Sleep well.'

As she left, the boy said, 'Mam!'

'Yes, Geordie?'

'Can I take some candles down the mine?' he begged.

The woman shook her head. 'They cost more than a penny every day! You'll spend most of your wages just on light!'

'Please mam!' Geordie asked. 'Just until I get used to the work.'

'All right! But just for one week and then no more!' she warned and blew her candle out.

35

II

Mister Wilson's boots clacked crisply on the cobbles while Geordie stumbled on and tried to stay in step.

'Am I to be a trapper?' Geordie panted.

'You are,' the man said briskly.

'What do trappers have to do?' the boy asked. 'Do they have to trap things?'

He stepped into the cage, crammed amongst the men, and gasped as it dropped suddenly into the blackness. The air rushed upwards, smelling hot and damp and choking Geordie. After half a minute the cage jolted to a stop. Geordie's knees were weaker than his cold tea.

He staggered out into the cave. The candles of the men sparkled in a line like a necklace of light as they set off along the tunnel.

'This is the horse-way,' Mister Wilson said.

Geordie nodded. Horses clattered past with wagons full of coal to load into the cage. 'So where do I work?' Geordie dared to ask.

'Another mile,' the tall man answered.

A mile! Geordie's little legs could never walk a mile! He trudged on after Mister Wilson. Men began to disappear down some passages that opened from the side walls of the horse-way. At last they were alone. The grey-faced overman pointed down a passage. 'Turn off down this barrow-way!'

The barrow-way was narrow and the darkest place that Geordie had ever been. Mister Wilson's candle glinted on the dark, damp walls and on the iron railway lines that ran along the floor.

At last the light shone on a wooden door. Mr Wilson turned and faced the boy. The candle shone up on his thin grey face, casting shadows in his tired red eyes. He pointed to the door.

'That's your trap!' the tall man said. 'You open it by pulling on this string. Here, try.'

Geordie pulled the string and watched the wood door open. 'It's there to keep the air out of the barrow-way. See?' the overman said.

'Yes,' young Geordie said, although he didn't really.

'The door has to stay closed,' the man went on. 'But of course it has to open when the trucks or barrows come along. That's your job – to open the door. And if a miner comes along and you aren't there and ready then he'll give you such a beating!' Mister Wilson warned.

'Is that what happened to our Tommy?' Geordie asked.

The man leaned forward and he peered hard in Geordie's face. 'No, lad. Tommy didn't wander off from duty. Tommy did a much worse thing!'

The young boy wondered what could be much worse. 'What was that?' he asked.

Mister Wilson spoke slowly and quite cruelly. 'What young Tommy Milburn did was simply fall asleep.'

'Fall asleep!' young Geordie squeaked. His mouth went dry. Fall asleep! The monster must have got him.

'He fell asleep. He fell asleep and fell across the line. The next time a truck came by, it . . . urrgh!' the tall man shuddered. He put his hand on Geordie's shoulder and led him to a little hole hacked in the side of the barrow-way wall. A hole no bigger than the kitchen fireplace far above in Geordie's home. 'You sit in here . . . now, take the string . . . the first truck should be down in half an hour.'

And then he left and took his candle with him. 'Mister Wilson!' Geordie called. His words just echoed off the empty walls. He had a pocket full of candles but nothing to light one with.

He sat there in the dark and he'd never felt so lonely in all his eight years.

38

His eyes grew used to the dark but he couldn't get used to the quietness. The odd drips of water made him jump. A steady thumping noise turned out to be his own heart. Sometimes the voices of men drifted to his door. But all the time he waited for the rattle and the roar of the great dark monster.

Geordie tried to sing a song he'd learned in Sunday school, but his dry mouth croaked a miserable sound and he gave up. He closed his tired eyes and thought about the Sunday school. The summer trips down to the river. The warm sun and the picnic food. He could smell the sweet grass and feel the cool water.

And the thoughts drifted into dreams as Geordie fell asleep! But when he'd fallen deep asleep the nightmare monster came to haunt him. He heard the rattle and the roar and then he thought he saw his Granny saying, 'Only boys who fall asleep! Only boys who fall asleep!'

He forced his tired eyes open. The rattle and the roar was real enough! His head was lying on the track and that whole track was shaking. Sparks were flying off the track and Geordie jerked his head back just in time. He hauled the string, the trap flew open and the heavy truck rushed by! 'Well done, young 'un!' a miner cried before he vanished in the black.

III

'They don't have monsters down the mine,' he told his granny as she tucked him in that night. 'They just have trucks that rush along.'

Granny Milburn nodded wisely. 'Sparking on the iron rails and rattling and a-roaring! That's what Tommy said. Just like monsters.'

'But still,' he yawned, 'that story saved my life! The nightmare woke me up in time! I'll never fall asleep again.'

Granny grinned and showed her pale pink gums. 'Yes you will,' she said. 'You'll fall asleep before the clock strikes ten!'

'I mean,' the boy began to murmur. 'I mean . . . at work. . . .'

The woman tucked his blanket in and ran her old hand through his new-washed hair. 'Sleep well,' she said.

Did you know. . . ?
In 1842 the law was changed. Children under ten years of age, and women, were no longer allowed to work in the mines.

Vile Victorian names

Victorian parents could be cruel to their children in many ways. For example, they could torture them for life by giving them a terrible name. Which of the following names were given to Victorian children?

ABISHAG?
FEATHER?
LETTUCE?
BRAINED?
SHEEPDOG?
HAM?
UZ?
CLAPHAM?
TRAM?
DESPAIR?
WATER?
KYLIE?
ENERGETIC?
MURDER?
WONDERFUL?

Answer: All are vile Victorian names except Kylie and Sheepdog.

Vile Victorian child labour . . . or, Wouldn't you rather stay at home?

Home life was not easy. With parents and elder brothers and sisters at work for most of the day, you could find yourself left at home to care for toddlers and babies. George Simms in 1881 describes a typical life of one such carer.

There she sat, in the bare squalid room, perched on a sack, erect, motionless, expressionless, on duty . . . left to guard a baby that lay asleep on the bare boards behind her, its head on its arm, the ragged remains of what had been a shawl flung over its legs.

Question: How old was this girl?
Answer: Four years old.

If you were not lucky enough to find work as a servant, or in the mines or factories, you could find other ways to earn your keep. Here are some examples. Which do you prefer?

Nail making

On average a child would earn three to four shillings a week if his nails were good quality. If not, he could expect a severe beating, or something much worse . . .

Somebody in the warehouse took him and put his head down on an iron counter and hammered a nail through his ear, and the boy has made good nails ever since.

Children's Employment Commission (1842)

Chimney sweeping
This was a popular job for young boys and girls, who were chosen for their size and agility.

Life was cruel and conditions were vile. Working in hot, dark and cramped conditions was very hard and tiring. Children often scraped their elbows and knees as they climbed up inside the chimneys. One sweep said...

No one knows the cruelty they undergo in learning. The flesh must be hardened. This is done by rubbing it, chiefly on the elbows and the knees, with the strongest brine (salt water) close by a hot fire. You must stand over them with a cane...

But beware! Any of you who think this job was easy, think again! If a worker was found sleeping on the job, or if by his own misfortune he became stuck in the chimney, his master would light a fire beneath him!

Ribbon making
You may think that making ribbons for the hair and the dresses of ladies was a pleasant, gentle occupation? Think again!

Three hundred boys were employed in turning hand looms. The endless whirl had such a bad effect on the head and the stomach that the little turners often suffered in the brain and the spinal chord and some died of it. In one mill near Cork six deaths and 60 mutilations have occurred in four years.

Victorian observer

Vile Victorian schools

So you have to go to school? Blame the Vile Victorians! In 1870 the Education Bill was passed. The aim was... *to bring education within the reach of every English home, aye, and within the reach of those children who have no homes.*

Children of the 1990s still suffer the horror of homework, the terror of teachers and the dread of school dinners. But, if you think school is bad in the 20th century, you should have gone to school in the 19th!

Here are four school sins. What punishment would you give for each one?

Make the punishment fit the crime

1 Throwing ink pellets in class, punished by...
a) A severe talking-to by the teacher
b) Kneeling on the floor with your hands behind your head
c) A treble helping of lumpy mashed potato at school dinner.

2 Missing Sunday church, punished by . . .
a) A severe talking-to by the priest and detention while you listen to the sermon you missed
b) A beating with a strap
c) Doing extra work for the church – polishing the candlesticks, digging a few graves, copying out the bible etc.

3 Being late for school, punished by . . .
a) Having your name written in the Punishment Book so you may not get a job when you leave school
b) Being hit over the hand with a cane
c) Both.

4 Ink blots and fingermarks on work, punished by . . .
a) Being caned (so your hands are sore and you probably make even more mess)
b) Having to do the work again
c) Death.

Answers:
1 b)   Kneeling
One punishment was to kneel on the hard, rough floorboards, with your back upright and your hands placed on the back of your neck for a long period of about twenty minutes. Should you lop over, aching all over, the teacher would slap you across the head with his hand and shout sternly, 'Get upright, will you?'

Victorian boy

2 b)   The strap
Every Monday morning the priest came to each class and asked us who had missed church the day before. I always had to miss Sunday because Sunday was washing day and we only had one lot of clothes. So, week by week we admitted our absence and were given the strap for it. We should have been able to explain but we were ashamed to give the real reason. Once, just once, I answered back.

  'Don't you know,' the priest said, 'that God loves you and wants to see you in His house on Sundays?'

  'But if he loves us, why does he want us to get the strap on Monday?' I asked.

  I don't remember what the priest said, but I do know I got a double load of stripes when he'd gone.

Victorian girl

3 c)   The punishment book
With no exams at the end of your school life, the chance of a good job after school depended on your final report – your reference. One boy was kept back by his father and so he was late for school . . .

The only boy in the school to be late. I was humiliated in front of three hundred boys by the headmaster and afterwards got six mighty slashes on the fingers with a thin cane. My God, it hurt, believe me. And something else which hurt even more. My name was inserted in the disgrace and punishment book and put on record for future reference.

                                              Victorian boy

4 a)   The cane
Some teachers chose specially thin canes because they hurt more. Many a time the cane would be broken over the hand (or bottom) of the pupil. Caning still went on in English schools more than eighty years after Victoria died. (Ask your parents!)

The terrible teachers' top ten facts

1 One of the most famous teachers in the 19th century was William Shaw. But he was famous for all the wrong reasons. Shaw was the headmaster of Bowes Academy in North Yorkshire. The writer Charles Dickens heard about Shaw when the headmaster's bad treatment landed him in court. Shaw was so cruel that two of his pupils lost their sight.

Dickens visited the school in 1837 and observed the man. He then created the villainous headmaster, Wackford Squeers, in his book *Nicholas Nickleby*. Everybody knew that Wackford Squeers was really William Shaw.

The publication of the book ruined Shaw's business. He died in 1850. Serves him right? End of story? Not quite. Some of the local people of Bowes thought that Dickens had been unfair to Shaw. They dedicated a window to Shaw in the local church after his death.

2 Some vile Victorian teachers didn't believe in talking to pupils to find out why they did something wrong. They simply punished them. Teachers had a motto . . .

For bad boys a yard of strap is worth a mile of talk.

I THINK IT'S THE OTHER WAY ROUND

3 Teachers could train by working in the classroom with an older teacher. Trainee teachers started at the age of 14.
4 Trainees could go to college. Some college rules were worse than school rules! At one men's college, the trainee teachers could . . .

> **not** leave the college except at certain times
> **not** go to the bedrooms during the day
> **not** stay up after 10:00 p.m.
> **not** have a light on in their bedroom
> **not** go to any public house
> **not** smoke
> **not** make friends with the local people

FUN, FUN, FUN

And they had to take some form of active exercise every afternoon!
5 The Victorians believed that boys should be treated differently from girls . . . and that men were more important than women. This showed in the schools.

In 1870, women teachers were paid 58 pounds a year . . . but men were paid 94!

Boys' lessons included carpentry, farmwork, gardening, shoe making, drawing, handicrafts.

Girls' lessons included housewifery (sweeping, dusting, making beds and bathing a baby), needlework and cookery.

6 Cookery lessons were difficult in poorer schools where pupils couldn't afford the ingredients. An inspector once made a report on a class of girls who had a lesson on roasting meat. One single chop was prepared and cooked by 18 girls!

7 Lessons were often just learning things by heart, then repeating them. A typical (horrible) history lesson went like this:

> WHO WAS HENRY THE EIGHTH?
>
> SON OF HENRY THE SEVENTH
>
> WHAT WAS HIS CHARACTER?
>
> AS A YOUNG MAN HE WAS GENEROUS ROYAL AND VERY HANDSOME
>
> HOW WAS HE WHEN HE GREW OLD?
>
> HE WAS FAT, VAIN CRUEL AND SELFISH!

8 Reading books were even worse! Children learned to read from books which had wonderful lines like . . .

Do not nod on a sod.
Can a ram sit on a sod?
Let Sam sip the sap of the red jam.

9 There were often as many as 70 or 80 pupils in one class. The teachers would have to shout or even scream to be heard above the noise of the children. One doctor had so many teachers complaining of sore throats he called it, 'Board School Laryngitis'!

10 Punishments were given in factories to get the most work possible from a child. One man, Joseph Lancaster, invented a similar system of punishments which was used in some schools. (They are quite vile, so please don't try them out on your teacher!)

'The log' A piece of wood weighing four to six pounds was tied across the shoulders of the offending child so that, when he moved, the log acted as a dead weight. It was a punishment for talking, which often didn't work, as the child would be in floods of noisy tears.

'Pillory and stocks' Unlike earlier times, children who suffered this 'pleasure' were not pelted by rotten tomatoes. They were put in the stocks, left and forgotten about.

'The cage' This was a basket suspended from the ceiling, into which the more serious offenders were put.

Vile Victorian schools – six of the best

Did you know...?

1 Many parents couldn't afford to send their children to the new Board Schools set up in the 1870s. It wasn't just the penny a week they had to pay – it was the fact that children weren't free to help their mothers with the housework, or earn the family extra money by working.

2 Some schools had special offers like, 'Three for the price of two'. If there were three children in a family at school, then the parents paid for the first two and the third could go free.

HOW MUCH FOR THIRTEEN?

3 Some parents blamed teachers for making the children go to school. One teacher wrote...
I well remember how, early in my career as a teacher, I had to avoid various missiles thrown at me by angry parents who would rather have the children running errands or washing up things in the home than wasting their time in school with such things as learning.

4 If a parent didn't want to send their child to school, they would say that the child was ill. A School Board Inspector would have to go to check if the 'illness' went on too long. One inspector was told that a child was dead – when he visited the house he found the 'dead' child was so well she was skipping in the middle of the living-room floor!

5 School Board Inspectors were so unpopular in some areas that they had to go around in pairs – to protect each other from angry parents!

6 School Dinners – 1885 style

MENU

PENNY DINNER
Boiled Pork, meat pudding, vegetables

FARTHING DINNER
Soup, bread and jam

FREE DINNER
Cup of cocoa or soup made from boiling meat bones

Vile Victorian fun and games

Some games you could try

Geordie bowling
Each competitor has a ball of clay the size of a tennis ball – or a rag ball, or a bean bag if you prefer.
1 Taking turns, throw your ball as far as you can.
2 Collect it and throw it again... and again... and again until you reach the end of the course. (Geordies threw them for a mile – you could try the length of your school playing field).
3 The one who reaches the end with the fewest throws is the winner.

Up the buttons
1 Everyone needs a collection of buttons (or counters) to play with. Make sure you can each identify which are your own.
2 Mark a large chalk square on the pavement near the wall of a house.
3 Mark the word 'OXO' in the centre.
4 Decide how many buttons each person is going to play (say 10).
5 Each player (say 6) places their buttons along the kerb in line with the square.
6 Take turns to flick each button forward (with thumb and finger).
7 After all the buttons have been flicked into the square, the player whose button is nearest the 'X' of the OXO is the winner.
8 The winner gathers up all the buttons.

Vile Victorian games you must never ever try!

1 Only the very rich had proper toilets with water to wash the contents into the sewers. The poor had to make do with a small building at the bottom of the yard. There was a wooden bench with a hole in it. Underneath were ashes from the fire. Once a week the ashes would be collected by Night Soil Men and taken away on a cart to be dumped.

But... some vile Victorian children took sticks and dipped them in the waste. They then carried the dirty sticks to the posher streets and wiped them on the door-knockers of the houses!

2 A popular trick was to tie two door-knockers together across the street, rap on the doors, then hide and watch as the two house owners struggled against each other to open the doors!

Some sports you would find very vile

Ratting
Bets are placed on how many rats a dog can kill in a given amount of time. The fight takes place in a large rat pit.

A 19th-century visitor describes a ratting event...

The floor was swept and a big, flat basket produced, like those in which chickens are brought to market. Under the top can be seen a small mound of closely packed rats. This match seemed to be between the rat-pit owner and his son. The bet was a bottle of lemonade. It was strange to watch the daring manner in which the lad pushed his hand into the rat cage and fumbled about and stirred up with his fingers the living mass, picking up only the big ones, as he'd been told.

When 50 animals had been flung into the pit they gathered themselves into a mound which reached one third up the sides. They were all sewer and water-ditch rats and the smell that rose from them was like that from a hot drain.

The moment the terrier was loose he buried his nose in the mound till he brought one out in his mouth. In a short time a dozen rats were lying bleeding on the floor and the white paint of the pit became grained with blood.

In a little time the terrier had a rat hanging on to his nose which, despite his tossing, still held on. He dashed up against the sides of the pit, leaving a patch of blood as if a strawberry had been smashed there.

'Time!' called the owner. The dog was caught and held, panting, his neck stretched out like a serpent's, staring at the rats that still kept crawling about.

The lad with the rats asked, 'Would any gentleman like any rats?'

Boxing

No gloves. No real rules, except you don't kick an opponent when they're on the ground. The winner is the one left standing at the end. Women's boxing was common. Large crowds would gather when a challenge was issued . . .

> 'I Elizabeth Wilkinson of Clerkenwell, having had angry words with Hannah Highfield, do invite her to meet me on the stage and box for three guineas. Each woman is to hold a half-crown coin in each hand. The first woman that drops her money loses the battle'.
>
> *E Wilkinson*

The reply came . . .

> 'I Hannah Highfield of Newgate Market, hearing the challenge of Elizabeth Wilkinson, will not fail, God willing, to give her more blows than words.'
>
> *H Highfield*

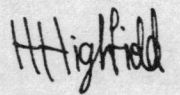

Vile Victorian sportsmen

The Eighth Earl of Bridgewater was fond of shooting. But when his eyesight began to fade, he had the wings of pigeons clipped to slow them down. That way they were easier to hit! But at least the Earl loved his dogs . . .

He had soft leather boots made for them to protect their paws.

He took half a dozen of them for rides in his carriage each day.

He dined with twelve of them every night in the great hall of his house.

Each dog had a clean white napkin round its neck. Servants stood behind them, dishing out food onto the family's silver plates while the Earl chatted to the dogs politely.

And if you think he was odd, what about the Second Baron Rothschild? He had a carriage drawn by four zebras. Snakes twined themselves around the bannisters of the stairway in his house.

FANCY AN APPLE?

A tame bear had a habit of slapping lady guests on the bottom. Twelve dinner guests found they had 12 beautifully dressed partners sitting next to them – they were monkeys!

A question of Victorian sport

1 Matthew Webb was the first man to achieve a great feat in 1875. The Mayor of Dover welcomed him and announced...

I make so bold as to say that I don't believe, in the future history of the world, any such feat will be performed by anybody else.

He was wrong! What did Matthew Webb do?

2 Blackburn Rovers had to play a soccer match against Burnley in 1891. It had been snowing for three hours before the game. The Blackburn team weren't too keen to turn out. By half time they were three goals down. For the second half only seven players bothered to leave the warmth of the dressing room.

Ten minutes later, Lofthouse, one of the Blackburn players, smacked the face of the Burnley captain. The Burnley captain hit him back. They were both sent off. The Blackburn players followed them – except the goalkeeper, Clegg. Burnley played on and scored. The Blackburn goalkeeper claimed the goal was offside. He was right. The referee abandoned the game.

But why had the Blackburn players walked off?

61

3 In 1885, in Scotland, the team Bon Accord stayed on the pitch even though they were losing ten-nil at half time. After the break they got tired and gave away even more goals. The final score is the greatest ever recorded in a professional soccer match.
What was that score?

4 In 1894, a cricket record was broken in Australia – the highest number of runs scored from a single ball. The ball was hit in the air and landed in the forked branch of a tree. The batsmen started to run. Two fielders climbed the tree. A branch snapped and they fell out. The batsmen ran on. The fielding team decided to chop the tree down – they wasted a lot of time looking for an axe. The batsmen ran on. The fielding team found some guns and shot the branches off the tree. By the time the ball fell to earth, the batting team had declared and had gone for tea. But how many runs had they scored?

5 The first cyclist to take a long-distance ride ended in Glasgow, where he knocked down a little boy in the street. He was taken to court and the magistrate fined him five shillings.
But who paid the fine?

6 The Duke of Beaufort liked to play 'real' (or indoor) tennis at his stately home. He played in the picture gallery of the house but gave up. The ball was wrecking the precious oil paintings on the walls. Instead he played a similar game but replaced the ball with something else. The game had been played in India, where it was known as Poona. But Victorian people who learned to play it named the game after the Duke of Beaufort's house. We still play The Duke's game today.
But what do we call it?

Answers:
1 He swam the English Channel.
2 They were cold.
3 Arbroath 36 – Bon Accord 0.
4 286 runs.
5 The magistrate! He thought the machine was so wonderful!
6 Badminton – of course! And the tennis ball was replaced by the shuttlecock.

Vile Victorian poems, plays and songs

If the Victorians had a favourite subject, then it was Death. There was nothing they liked better than a sad story of suffering, heartbreak, tragedy and cruelty. The trouble was it was not just the subjects that were painful. The writing was pretty bad too! The Victorian ballad writers were probably the world's worst poets.

Vile Victorian love songs

No radio or television, no records or tapes. How did the Victorians entertain themselves at home? The middle classes would buy a piano, learn to play it and then sing some songs. Love songs were as popular then as they are today, but can you imagine standing by the family piano and singing this?

> **That is Love**
> *See the father standing at his cottage door,*
> *Watching the baby in the gutter rolling o'er,*
> *Laughing at his merry pranks, but hark! A roar!*
> *Help! Oh, help him! Gracious Heav'n above!*
> *Dashing down the road there comes a maddened horse!*
> *Out the father rushes with resistless force.*
> *Saves the child . . . but he lies there, a mangled corpse.*
> *That is love, that is love!*

If that's not cheerful enough for you, then you may prefer a children's song. The moral of the song is that death's not really that bad if you've behaved yourself in this life . . .

Shall I be an Angel, Daddy?
One day a father to his little son
Told a sad story, a heart-breaking one,
He took from an album a photo, and said,
'This is your mother, but she's been long dead;
You she has left me to cherish and love,
She is an angel, my child, up above.'
The boy in an instant drew close to his side,
And these are the words that he softly replied . . .

Chorus:
Shall I be an angel, daddy?
An angel in the sky?
Will I wear the golden wings,
And rest in peace on high?
Shall I live forever and ever
With the angels fair?
If I go to heaven, oh! tell me, Daddy,
Will I see Mother there?

Are the tears running down your legs? Or do you just feel sick? Perhaps you'd be better getting out of the house and going to the theatre.

Vile Victorian plays

The theatres were very popular. So popular that they built huge ones to fit all the people in. If your seat was at the back, then you were a long way from the actors, of course. Never mind. The actors shouted all their lines and made huge gestures with their hands. In fact they over-acted like mad so that everyone got the point.

The plays were written to match this style. Simple plots and characters. Baddies were bad and goodies were good. You booed and hissed the villain and cheered for the hero. This style of theatre was known as 'Melodrama'. Songs were mixed with the action.

And the messages were simple too. In *Ten Nights in a Bar-Room*, written by William W. Pratt in 1858, the message was simply, 'Don't drink alcohol.' Here is the most touching scene – have a tissue handy to wipe away your tears . . .

SCENE: Interior of the *Sickle and Sheaf* Public House. Joe Morgan is drinking with his friends, including Simon Slade, the landlord. Little Mary Morgan is outside the door.

Mary: (Crying) Father! Father! Where is my father? (Enter Mary – she runs to Morgan)
Oh! I've found you, at last! Now won't you come home with me?
Morgan: Blessings on thee, my little one! Darkly shadowed is the sky that hangs gloomily over thy young head.
Mary: Come, father, mother has been waiting a long time, and I left her crying so sadly. Now do come home and make us all so happy.
Mary: (singing)
Father, dear father, come home with me now!
The clock in the steeple strikes one.
You promised, dear father, that you would come home
As soon as your day's work was done;
Our fire has gone out – our house is all dark –
And mother's been watching since tea,
With poor brother Benny so sick in her arms,
And no one to help her but me.

Chorus:
Come home, come home, come home,
Please father, dear father, come home.
Hear the sweet voice of the child,
Which the night winds repeat as they roam!
Oh! Who could resist this most plaintive of prayers?
Please, father, dear father, come home.

Father, dear father, come home with me now!
The clock in the steeple strikes two;
The night has grown colder and Benny is worse –
But he has been calling for you.
Indeed he is worse – Ma says he will die,
Perhaps before morning shall dawn;
And this is the message she sent me to bring:
'Come quickly or he will be gone.'

Chorus:
Come home . . .

Father, dear father, come home with me now!
The clock in the steeple strikes three;
The house is so lonely – the hours are so long
For poor weeping mother and me.
Yes, we are alone – poor Benny is dead,
And gone with the angels of light;
And these were the very last words that he said –
'I want to kiss Papa goodnight!'

Chorus:
Come home . . .

Morgan: (Suddenly realising the evil of his drinking habit)
Yes, my child, I'll go. (Kisses her) You have robbed me of my last penny, Simon Slade, but this treasure still remains. Farewell, friend Slade. (To Mary) Come, dear one, come. I'll go home. Come, come! I'll go, yes, I'll go.
(Exit Morgan and Mary)

Happy ending – except for poor Benny, of course? No chance. Later in the drama, a glass is thrown at Morgan. It misses him – and hits little Mary on the head instead. She dies while singing a hymn to her grief-stricken parents. As Morgan collapses on the couch and Mrs Morgan sobs over the body, the curtain falls.

NOW the Victorian audience could go home happy! They could also go to the pub. In London, one house in every 77 was reckoned to be a public house. In part of Newcastle, there was one pub for every 22 families.

Mr Morgan could well have drunk a lot of beer. Dishonest landlords like Slade would add salt to the beer, so the more you drank the thirstier you got! (Today they have crisps and peanuts instead!)

Vile Victorian books

But it wasn't just the popular writers who loved sentimental mush. The 'serious' writers were at it too. The ones your teachers call 'Classical' – people like Charles Dickens...

The Old Curiosity Shop

(The boy Kit has come to visit his friend Little Nell. She's as dead as a rocking-horse's hoof, but her aged father doesn't want to believe it.)

'Where is she?' demanded Kit. *'Oh tell me but that – but that, dear master!'*

'She is asleep – yonder – in there.'*

'Thank God!'

'Ay! Thank God!' returned the old man. *'I have prayed to him many, and many, and many a livelong night, when she has been asleep. She is sleeping soundly,'* he said; *'but no wonder. Angel hands have strewn the ground deep with snow so that the lightest footsteps may be lighter yet; and even the birds are dead so that they may not wake her.** She used to feed them. The timid things would fly from us. They never flew from her.'*

Kit had no power to speak. His eyes were filled with tears.***

For she was dead.**** There upon the little bed she lay at rest.

She was dead. No sleep so beautiful and calm, so free from trace of pain, so fair to look upon.

She was dead. Dear, gentle, patient, noble Nell was dead.

Where were the traces of her early cares, her sufferings, her fatigues? All gone.

And still her former self lay there. Yes. The old fireside had smiled upon that same sweet face. At the still bedside of the dying boy there had been the same mild, lovely look. So shall we see the angels in their majesty after death.

The old man looked in agony to those who stood around as if imploring them to help her. She was dead, and past all help or need of it.

She had been dead two days.

* Being dead as a duck's toe nail she will get one heck of a shock when she tries to wake up.
** But not as dead as Little Nell!
*** He's guessed!
**** I told you so!

Vile Victorian poetry

And the most respected of Victorian poets, Alfred, Lord Tennyson, the Poet Laureate. His most popular poem was *In Memoriam*, written in memory of his dead friend, Arthur. Queen Victoria loved it! It drones on for hundreds and hundreds of verses about death. Verses like...

> *I sing to him that rests below,*
> *And, since the grasses round me wave,*
> *I take the grasses of the grave,*
> *And make them pipes whereon to blow.*

Can you imagine that... taking grass off a grave to make a pipe to play?

At least some Victorian poets could laugh at the serious ones with hilarious poems that made fun of the tragic ones...

Mr Jones by Harry Graham (1899)
'There's been an accident!' they said,
'Your servant's cut in half; he's dead!'
'Indeed!' said Mr Jones, 'and please
Send me the half that's got my keys.'

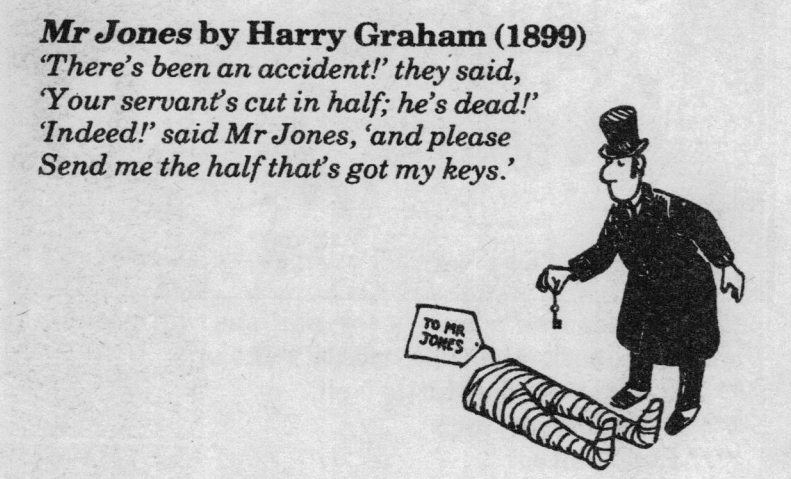

Vile Victorian life

The industrial revolution

FACTORY WORK INCREASED
SO...
PEOPLE MOVED IN GREAT NUMBERS FROM THE COUNTRY TO WORK IN THE TOWNS
SO...
MORE PEOPLE MEANT MORE HOUSES
SO...
BUILDERS COULD NOT KEEP UP WITH THIS DEMAND
SO...
INSTEAD OF BECOMING HOMELESS, POOR PEOPLE SHARED THIER HOUSES WITH MANY OTHERS
SO...
THIS LED TO SERIOUS OVERCROWDING
SO...
YOUR HOME HAD TO BE NEAR TO YOUR PLACE OF WORK
SO...
MANY HOUSES WERE NEAR TO FOUL-SMELLING CANALS, RIVERS, RAILWAY-LINES, SMOKING FACTORY CHIMNEYS AND EVEN SEWERS
SO...
YOU HAD AN UNHEALTHY LIFE
SO
YOU DIED!

The Corn Law revolution

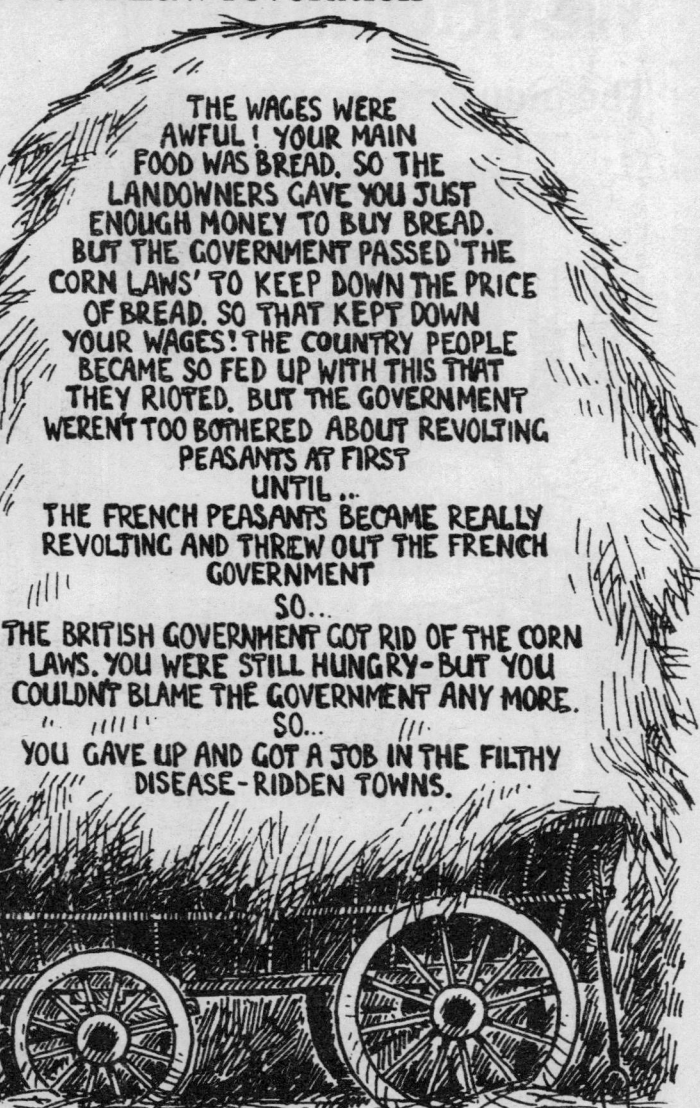

THE WAGES WERE AWFUL! YOUR MAIN FOOD WAS BREAD, SO THE LANDOWNERS GAVE YOU JUST ENOUGH MONEY TO BUY BREAD. BUT THE GOVERNMENT PASSED 'THE CORN LAWS' TO KEEP DOWN THE PRICE OF BREAD. SO THAT KEPT DOWN YOUR WAGES! THE COUNTRY PEOPLE BECAME SO FED UP WITH THIS THAT THEY RIOTED. BUT THE GOVERNMENT WEREN'T TOO BOTHERED ABOUT REVOLTING PEASANTS AT FIRST

UNTIL...

THE FRENCH PEASANTS BECAME REALLY REVOLTING AND THREW OUT THE FRENCH GOVERNMENT

SO...

THE BRITISH GOVERNMENT GOT RID OF THE CORN LAWS. YOU WERE STILL HUNGRY – BUT YOU COULDN'T BLAME THE GOVERNMENT ANY MORE.

SO...

YOU GAVE UP AND GOT A JOB IN THE FILTHY DISEASE-RIDDEN TOWNS.

1 Carter   2 Blacksmith   3 Pedlar
4 Mower   5 Milkmaid
6 Mole-catcher 7 Shepherd.

75

Ten foul facts on vile Victorian towns

1 All the sewage of Cambridge used to flow into the river, which made it a pretty disgusting place to walk beside. In 1843, Queen Victoria was walking beside the river when she asked one of the university teachers an embarrassing question.

2 In 1853 a cholera epidemic in London killed 11,500. London's drains carried sewage and germs straight into the river Thames. The river water was then used for washing clothes and even cooking! The Thames was such a stinking sewer in the hot summer of 1858 that the blinds of the Houses of Parliament had to be soaked in chloride of lime so that the MPs could meet without choking on the smell.

3 Until the mid 1860s, London relied on water pumped from the river Thames as its main source. But up to 200 sewers emptied into it! Raw sewage could be seen coming out of standpipes in the streets of London, and out of kitchen taps in the houses of the rich, the water flowed a 'healthy' brown colour! In London, an Inspector in 1847 discovered that sewage was a problem which would not go away on its own. He reported ...

The filth was lying scattered around the rooms, vaults, cellars and yards, so thick and so deep, that it was hardly possible to move through it.

4 Some men were given the job of clearing rubbish from the river Thames ... and for recovering dead bodies. There was a reward for finding a missing person, but the Thames body-finders had an extra reward – they stripped the body of its valuables. As Dickens said in *Our Mutual Friend* ...

Has a dead body any use for money? Is it possible for a dead man to have money? Can a corpse own it, want it, spend it, claim it, miss it?

5   The Victorian poor were known affectionately as 'The Great Unwashed'. Why? There was very little water in the poorer areas of town. What there was had to be taken from a standpipe in the street – when it was available. What little water they had was barely enough to cook with, so to save it they went without a wash!

6   The Victorian dead were more important than the living poor! When St Pancras Station was built, the railway company had to put a line through a graveyard. They had to contact the relatives of the dead and pay the costs of doing whatever the relatives wanted. But the homes of thousands of poor people were flattened – the railway company didn't have to pay them a penny!

7   Drainage was not introduced in London until 1865. Until then, water from sinks and makeshift toilets ran down old sewers into the Thames, or drained into huge cesspools under houses.

8 The Metropolitan Underground railway line opened in 1863 – steam trains pulled open trucks at first. In 1887, R. D. Blumenfeld wrote . . .

The compartment in which I sat was filled with passengers who were smoking pipes, as is the British habit, and as the smoke and sulphur filled the tunnel, all the windows have to be closed. The atmosphere was a mixture of sulphur, coal dust and foul fumes from the oil lamp above; so that by the time we reached Moorgate Street I was near dead of asphyxiation and heat. I should think these Underground railways must soon be discontinued, for they are a menace to health.

9 A report on the Borough of Tynemouth revealed the following in 1851 . . .

Eleven persons had been living in this house for a long time with no other means than thieving. They were feeding themselves with a piece of roast beef, eggs, tea and some hot whisky. The rooms of the house were in the most filthy condition that can be imagined; it beggars description. In one of the cupboards, having occasion to search there for some stolen property, there was a deposit of human filth; there were four beds in the room, three persons to a bed; behind the beds was a hen roost with a deposit of filth; the smell from the room was most overpowering. Connecting that room with the one above was a trapdoor by which a person could escape from one room to another when pursued by the police.

10 One of Victoria's least favourite towns was Newcastle. In 1850 she went there to open the new high level railway bridge. The London to Edinburgh rail link was now complete and she could travel from London to her summer holiday palace in Scotland without a break. She ought to have been pleased.

But, the story goes, a celebration banquet for the opening of the bridge was held in the Station Hotel in Newcastle. Before Victoria left, the manager of the hotel presented her with the bill for the banquet.

The Queen was furious! She vowed never to look upon the town again. For the next 50 years she drew the curtains on her railway carriage every time she passed through.

(But she allowed Newcastle 'Town' to become a 'City' in 1882.)

And even if you escaped to the fresh air of the Victorian countryside your life could still be very vile.

Vile Victorian work

Small clothing factories were known as sweatshops. To save money the workers were crammed into a small room, often a basement with no light or fresh air. To press the clothes that the women made, the tailor heated an iron on a gas or coke fire. The room was full of steam and the air was full of choking dust from the cloth. The wages in the 1890s could be as low as three shillings (15p) a week. Thomas Hood wrote this poem in 1843 about the girls who sewed shirts.

The Song of the Shirt

With fingers weary and worn
With eyelids heavy and red,
A woman sat in unwomanly rags
Plying her needle and thread –

Stitch! stitch! stitch!
In poverty, hunger and dirt.

Work–work–work
Till the brain begins to swim;
Work–work–work
Till the eyes are heavy and dim;
Till over the buttons I fall asleep
And sew them on in my dreams!

Oh men with sisters dear,
Oh men with mothers and wives,
It is not linen you're wearing out
But human creatures' lives
Stitch! Stitch! Stitch!
In poverty hunger and dirt,
Sewing at once with a double thread
A shroud as well as a shirt.

Thomas Hood

Vile Victorian factory work

True or false?
Rules for the factory workers were as bad as school rules. Which of the following facts were true for workers in Victorian factories?

1 There was to be no breathing between the hours of 9 a.m. and 5 p.m.
True/False

2 There was a fine for whistling or singing while you work.
True/False

3 Start work at 6 a.m. but no breakfast until 8 a.m.
True/False

4 There was a rule against losing fingers in the machinery.
True/False

5 There was a fine for talking with anyone outside your own line of work.
True/False

6 Anyone dying at work would be sacked on the spot.
True/False

7 The managers would alter the clocks so you'd be late for work. Then they'd fine you for your lateness.
True/False

8 No young children to be brought by parents into the factory.
True/False

9 'Mould runners' – child workers in the Midland potteries – worked for 12 hours in temperatures of 100–120°F/35–40°C.
True/False

10 Boy labourers worked for chainsmiths and used huge hammers. This gave them powerful, muscular bodies.
True/False

Answers:
1 False – not even the Victorians were that bad!
2 True – whistling or singing disturbed the other workers, the managers said.
3 True – 30 to 40 minutes were allowed for breakfast, one hour for lunch and 20 minutes for tea.
4 False – there was no actual rule against losing a finger, but it was one of the most common forms of accident. Less common, but still possible and even more vile, was the loss of a hand or arm; because of infection this could easily lead to death.
5 True – in some factories it was forbidden to talk to anyone at all!
6 False – but you wouldn't get much more than a minute's silence for your death; children had very little chance of getting payment for the death of a parent.
7 True – this was known to happen; there were once 95 workers locked out of a weaving mill; each one was fined three pence.
8 False – parents often took their children to help with their work; they were free labour for the factory owners.
9 True.
10 False – their frail bodies were twisted and crippled for life.

At least the Victorians improved life a little from the bad days of the early 1800s. The 1833 Factory Act cut the working day to 'only' ten hours if you were under 18 years old – and 'only' 48 hours a week if you were under 13. And the under-13s had to attend school, the law said. The trouble was there were usually no schools for them to attend!

The vile Victorian way of life and death

Life was hard and the death rate was very high. In Manchester, children and their parents were working 12 hour shifts in the factories and mills. If you were a child there was a good chance you wouldn't reach the age of 17, due to overwork, lack of food or the poisonous air which was all around you.

> LIFE'S NOT SO BAD SON... IF THEY DON'T WORK YER TOO MUCH, AND A MACHINE DON'T KILL YER, AND YER DON'T STARVE, AND YER DON'T GET POISONED, OR FROZEN, OR DISEASED, OR SACKED, OR CRIPPLED OR IN DEBT, OR PUT IN PRISON, OR...

Accidents in the factories were common, but many died before they were old enough to work. In Manchester, in the 1830s, over half of the number of children who died were only five years old! An official report on the death of a woman living in one room with her husband and son, shows the suffering of those living in slums.

She lay dead beside her son upon a heap of feathers which were scattered over her naked body, there being neither sheet nor coverlet. The feathers stuck so fast over the whole body that the physician could not examine the body until it was cleansed. Even then he found it starved and scarred from bites of vermin. Part of the floor of the room was torn up and the hole used by the family as a privy (toilet).

Ten things you always wanted to know about a pauper's funeral:

The Victorians' obsession with death went so far that families would rather starve than miss one payment towards the cost of their burial. Those who died without burial club money would face the disgrace of ... a pauper's funeral!

Would you fancy one?

1 They were free.
2 You'd be buried in a public graveyard ... at the back somewhere, where you would never be found, as ...
3 Paupers' graves didn't have headstones.
4 A headstone was 1p extra.
5 You wouldn't have a grave all to yourself.
6 You would share your grave with other dead paupers.
7 It was common for a pauper to share with more than 20 other bodies!
8 Burial grounds became so full with paupers' graves, that the bodies started to poke through the earth's surface, letting off a vile stench.
9 Grave diggers often had to jump up and down on the bodies in the mass graves, so that they could squeeze more bodies into them.
10 As for a religious funeral service ... there wasn't one.

Perhaps you'd hope a doctor could cure you before you died? Not if it was a vile Victorian doctor like Dr Meyers of Sheffield. He invented a wonderful cure for tapeworms in the stomach – a 'Tapeworm Trap'. It was a small metal cylinder tied to a piece of string. Some food was placed in the cylinder as 'bait'. To make the tapeworm hungry the patient had to starve himself for a few days. The trap was then swallowed. The starving tapeworm would pop its head into the cylinder where it would be caught with a metal spring. The trap would then be hauled back up with the tapeworm – in theory.

Dr Meyers had to stop selling this brilliant invention. The tapeworms weren't killed... but the patients were!! They choked to death on the traps!

Weird Victorian superstitions

The Victorians claimed to be Christians but they had a lot of superstitions that were definitely un-Christian. Can you match each superstitious action with its consequence?

Warning – the following can be damaging to your health

1 Placing new shoes on the table
2 Rocking an empty cradle
3 Planting yellow flowers in the garden
4 Putting a garment on inside-out
5 Swallowing a spider in butter
6 Throwing the first Shrove Tuesday pancake to the hens
7 Drinking elderberry juice
8 Killing a spider
9 Turning your money over in your pocket while staring at a new moon
10 Planting a leek somewhere on the house (the porch-roof or a cranny)

OI! WATCH WHERE YOU'RE THROWING THOSE PANCAKES!

What will happen
a) Brings good luck
b) Will give you plenty of eggs for the rest of the year
c) Means the wearer will die within the year
d) Is a powerful charm against warts
e) Brings bad luck
f) Makes sure the family will be protected from witches
g) Prevents the house from catching fire
h) Will double your money
i) Is a cure for whooping cough
j) Means there is a baby on the way

Answers: 1 = c) 2 = j) 3 = f) 4 = a) 5 = i) 6 = b) 7 = d) 8 = e) 9 = h) 10 = g)

Most superstitious of all was the composer Schoenberg. He was born on 13 September 1874. He believed that he would die on the 13th of a month. Since the numbers 6 and 7 add up to 13, he believed that he would die at the age of 76. He died in 1951 on Friday 13 July. Of course, that made him 76!

Vile Victorian food

Vile Victorian eating habits

Frank Buckland, a naturalist, and his father, Dr William Buckland, had a taste for trying unusual food.

True or false?
The Bucklands ate . . .

Elephant trunk	True/False
Roast giraffe	True/False
A mole	True/False
Stewed bluebottles	True/False
Alligator	True/False
Mice on toast	True/False
Squirrel pie	True/False
Mice in batter	True/False
The mummified heart of Louis XIV	True/False
Roast ostrich	True/False

Answer: All are vile but true! Dr William said that the mole was the worst thing he'd ever tasted, followed by the stewed bluebottles. Frank tried, but hated, fried earwigs. Yeuch!

Did you know...?
The Sanitary Commission of 1855 found...

- STARCH AND FLOUR IN COCOA
- RED LEAD AND OCHRE IN CAYENNE PEPPER
- AS MUCH AS 50 PER CENT ADDED WATER IN MILK
- INSECTS AND FUNGI IN SUGAR
- COPPER CONTAMINATION IN PRESERVED FRUITS
- CHLORATE OF LEAD IN CONFECTIONARY
- ALUM IN BREAD (SO IT WOULD HOLD WATER AND WEIGH MORE)

DID YOU ENJOY YOUR LUNCH DEAR?

Vile Victorian food for you to try

Here are some recipes you might like to try. The Victorians ate them. They won't harm you and you may even like them!

Candied Carrots

You will need
- 500g carrots
- 2 tablespoons golden syrup
- 2 tablespoons butter
- Chopped mint
- Salt

Now...

1. Use small carrots or larger carrots sliced length-wise. Boil in salted water until tender.
2. Melt the syrup and butter together in a pan.
3. Add the carrots, cook for ten minutes, stirring regularly.
4. Serve sprinkled with chopped mint.
5. Serves four. Ideal with the Sunday roast lamb.

On the other hand, if you want to eat like a **poor** Victorian, then you might like to try this recipe from Mrs Beeton. She said it was ...

seasonable at any time, especially during hard times, using whatever ingredients are available.

Half Pay Pudding

You Will Need
- 250g suet
- 125g breadcrumbs
- 250g flour
- A handful of currants and raisins
- 2 tablespoons treacle
- half pint of milk (minimum)

Now
1. Put the suet and flour in a mixing bowl and rub in thoroughly.
2. Add raisins and currants, and mix.
3. Slowly add the milk, stirring continuously until the mixture is thick and smooth.
4. Add treacle and stir well.
5. Place in a greased, oven-proof bowl and gently sprinkle breadcrumbs on the top.
6. Cook in a moderate oven until risen and breadcrumbs become toasted.
7. Serves all the family – but the more there are the less you get!

Vile Victorian facts

Test your teacher

1   Robert Peel (1788 - 1850) was famous for what?
a) Bringing the first oranges into the country – and that's where we get the phrase 'orange peel';
b) Founding the first police force – that's why they were called 'Peelers';
c) Being the first man to swim the English Channel blindfolded.

2   Florence Nightingale was so ill when she got back from nursing in the Crimean War (1854 - 6) that she spent the rest of life in bed. But in 1890 she managed to . . .?
a) Have tea with the Queen.
b) Take part in a charity fun run.
c) Record her voice on Edison's new machine.

3   William Schwenck Gilbert (1836 - 1911), the writer of the most popular Victorian comic operas, died at the age of 75. How did he die?
a) Drowning in his own pond trying to rescue a girl?
b) On stage during a performance of his last opera?
c) Choking on a chicken bone at a party to celebrate his latest success?

4 Who wrote the dreadful lines of poetry, describing a pond:

I've measured it from side to side;
'Tis three feet long and two feet wide.?

a) Famous Victorian poet, William Wordsworth (1770 - 1850);
b) Comic opera writer, W S Gilbert (1836 - 1911), in *The Pirates of Penzance*;
c) Queen Victoria in her diaries.

5 Victorians thought it was rude to use the word 'leg'. Instead they used the word:

a) Unmentionable – as in, 'We are having a lamb's unmentionable for Sunday lunch.'
b) Limb – as in, 'He's only pulling your limb, Jim.'
c) That-which-you-walk-on – as in, 'You put your right That-which-you-walk-on in, you put your left That-which-you-walk-on out, in out, in out, shake it all about.'

6 A Victorian husband had the legal right to do which of the following?

a) Lock up his wife;
b) Beat his wife;
c) Own all his wife's belongings, clothes and money.

Answers:

1b) Created the police force in 1829. Fell off his horse and died 21 years later, probably while exceeding the speed limit.

2c) The recording was made at her home on a cylinder.

3a) He was teaching the girl to swim at the time!

4a) He also wrote the famous *Daffodils* poem. He wandered round the Lake District with his sister, Dorothy, writing poems. During the French war in 1797 they were suspected of being spies, making notes for the enemy!

5b) Some Victorians even covered the legs of tables and chairs so that ladies wouldn't be shocked by the sight of a naked leg! And instead of having to say the shocking word 'trousers', some ladies preferred to call them 'the southern necessity'.

6a) b) and c): a) until 1891, b) until 1879, c) until 1882.

> MY POOR POOR HUSBAND TRIPPED OVER THE UNMENTIONABLE OF THE CHAIR, HURT HIS THAT-WHICH-YOU-WALK-ON, AND PUT A RIP IN HIS SOUTHERN NECESSITIES

Mad Victorian guide to travel

The richer Victorians were very keen on travel and exploration. They travelled the world to stop themselves from becoming bored at home. They massacred African wildlife to bring back lion-skin rugs, and they robbed poor countries of their historical treasures to fill our museums. Most travellers had servants to make life abroad as comfortable as life at home. But if you were brave enough to face foreign parts alone, there were guide books to help you.

Mad Victorian scientist, Francis Galton, published a book in 1855 called *The Art of Travel*. He suggested a cure if you felt unwell as you travelled in foreign countries.

Drop a little gunpowder into a glass of warm, soapy water and drink it. It will tickle the throat, but clear the system.

Sir Francis had other good travel hints that you may like to copy. What solutions would you come up with for these problems?
1   How could you light your pipe while out riding in a strong wind?
2   How would you keep your clothes dry in a tropical storm?
3   How would you soothe blisters on your feet?
4   How would you stop your brain from overheating with hard work (like in a horrible history lesson!)?
5   How would you cure a wasp sting?

Answers:

1   Get your horse to lie down and then use it as a wind shield, of course.

2   Take them off and sit on them until the rain stops! (Why didn't you think of that, eh? Maybe Sir Francis wasn't so mad after all!)

3   Make a lather of soap bubbles to fill your socks then break a raw egg into each boot. (Okay – maybe he was a few fruit cakes short of a picnic after all.)

4   Have a hat with holes in to let the air circulate. (Sir Francis had one with shutters so he could open or close the holes whenever he needed to.)

5   Take the gunge from your pipe and rub it into the sting.

The vile Victorian Army

The vile Victorians set out to conquer the world. When they defeated another country they could take its wealth, and its natural resources (diamonds from South Africa, sugar from the West Indies, cotton from Egypt, tea from India and so on). The Victorians back in England could make even bigger fortunes by trading with the conquered countries.

To conquer these countries Victorian Britain needed an army. Queen Victoria was very proud of her army. The army was pretty proud of itself. And that's surprising, because they weren't very good.

Did you know... or foul facts about the Victorians at war

1 Flogging of soldiers, long abolished on the continent, continued in the British army till 1881.

2 The British commander during the Crimean war was Lord Raglan. He was already rather senile at the age of 67. He had fought against the French in the Napoleonic wars about 40 years before. He insisted on calling the enemy, 'The French'. The enemy were the Russians – the French were on Raglan's side in the Crimea. No wonder he lost his Light Brigade!

3 The vile Victorian poets didn't just write about love and nature. They enjoyed writing about war too. Adam Linsay Gordon (1833 - 1870) had all the talent of a five-year-old, but published this epic on war...

Flash! Flash! bang! bang! and we blazed away,
And the grey roof reddened and rang;
Flash! Flash! and I felt his bullet flay
The tip of my ear. Flash! bang!

4 The poets did have their uses in war, though. In 1857, during the Indian Mutiny, piles of books were used as a defence. Byron's *Complete Poems* was almost destroyed but at least it stopped a cannonball.

5 During the Second Boer War in South Africa, Queen Victoria ordered tins of chocolate to be sent to each of her 'dear, brave soldiers'. A bullet hit Private James Humphrey's tin and saved his life.

IT'S PRIVATE HUMPHEY'S IDEA SIR

6 The Second Boer War (1899 - 1902) was fought in South Africa against the Dutch settlers who thought the land was theirs. This time the British weren't fighting against natives with spears – they were fighting determined settlers armed with German guns. And they didn't do very well. The British wore red uniform jackets – this made them easy targets – but at least they didn't show the blood. One of Victoria's 'dear brave soldiers' was badly wounded in the face by a piece of shell. He had been lying for hours, wounded, on a hillside. At last he was rescued. His face was too badly torn for him to speak. He signalled for a piece of paper to write on. The nurses thought he was going to ask for something vital. But he slowly, painfully wrote just three words. 'Did we win?' They nodded tearfully . . . nobody had the heart to tell him the British had lost!

DOES HE MEAN THE ARMY OR TOTTENHAM HOTSPUR?

7 The British lost many men in the First Boer War against a group of farmers and boys. At the Battle of Majuba Hill the British lost 93 soldiers. 133 were wounded and 58 captured. The Boer farmers lost just one person and five were wounded. One of the British dead was their leader, General Sir George Colley. Victoria sighed, 'Poor Sir George,' when she heard he'd been shot in the head . . . shot by a twelve-year-old boy!

8 Bobbie was a little mongrel dog and a tragic hero of the Afghan war. In 1880 his master was killed and the dog escaped to the British headquarters at Kandahar. His wounds were bandaged and he was taken back to England to be presented to Queen Victoria and receive his Afghan Medal from her. Having lived through the Afghan war it was a bit sad that he was shortly afterwards run over by a hansom cab and killed. He was stuffed and placed in a glass case (with his medal). He can be seen in the regiment's museum in Reading today.

9 The Indian Mutiny of 1857 was particularly vicious. As well as losing many lives in the mutiny, the Indians lost their nation's wealth. The British troops who captured Delhi began to loot it. One

group stole a golden wine cup studded with diamonds. They decided to give it to their lieutenant. They reckoned he could sell it and use the money to but himself a promotion to captain. He sold it in London. It turned out to be one of the most valuable Indian treasures ever seen. The lieutenant sold it for £80,000 (or more than a million pounds today) and he became one of the richest men in England!

> WE ROBBED THE INDIANS OF THEIR CUP...
> AND GAVE IT TO OUR LIEUTENANT.
> WHO SOLD IT, KEPT THE MONEY AND GOT FILTHY RICH...
> YEAH... WE WERE ROBBED

It wasn't only the vile Victorian army that got things wrong. In the American Civil War, General John Sedgwick looked over the top of his troops' defences at the battle of Spotsylvania in 1864. He scoffed at his men for hiding behind the defences. His last words were, 'They couldn't hit an elephant at this distan . . .!' Splatt! Bullseye!

> PITY HE WASN'T AN ELEPHANT

> BLEED BLEED

The world's shortest war

But... the British Navy wasn't quite so bad. In 1896 the British Battle fleet was sent to Zanzibar. Said Khalid was trying to take over the country and the British wanted him out.

1 Rear Admiral Rawson told Said to get out of the palace by 9:00 a.m. Said refused.
2 At 9:02 fighting broke out.
3 By 9:40 it was all over. It was one of the shortest battles in the history of the world.
4 The only Zanzibar warship, an old British steamer called *The Glasgow*, was sunk with two shells.
5 The palace was destroyed.
6 But the British navy hadn't finished making the locals suffer. They sent a bill to the people of Zanzibar, asking them to pay for the shells used to wreck the place!

Fifteen foul things that Florence found – or, Flit on cheering angel

Florence Nightingale became a legend for her nursing work during the Crimean War in Russia. She visited Scutari hospital in 1854 and reported back the terrible conditions...

1   The men can lie in filth for two weeks before being seen by a doctor.
2   The men are lying on unwashed floors.
3   The floors are crawling with vermin and insects.
4   One visiting priest left, covered in lice.
5   Few men have blankets or pillows...
6   ...they rest their heads on their boots and use overcoats for blankets.
7   Operations are carried out in the ward in full view of everyone.
8   The screams of the men having limbs cut off is terrible.
9   I had screens put around the operations – but they couldn't shut out the sound.
10 There are 1000 men in one hospital, many with diarrhoea.
11 There are just 20 chamber pots between them.
12 The toilets overflow onto the floor.
13 Men without shoes or slippers must paddle through this.
14 Amputated limbs are dumped outside to be eaten by dogs.
15 Men are surviving the battles and being killed by the hospitals!

Did You Know...?
Rearrange the letters of FLIT ON CHEERING ANGEL and you get FLORENCE NIGHTINGALE!

The vilest Victorian victory ... or, I'm dying to attack those cannon!

The Victorian Army won a few battles – somehow! But their most famous battle was at Balaclava – that's right, it was so cold they had to invent knitted helmets to keep out the cold. Balaclava helmets. (To tell the truth there was another old knit in charge of the Light Brigade – Lord Cardigan! Honest!)

Anyway, Lord Lucan was in charge of the cavalry – soldiers on horses – when they fought the famous Charge of the Light Brigade. The Queen's poet, Lord Tennyson, even wrote a popular poem telling what heroes they were. But were they brave or were they batty? Make up your own mind ...

The charge of the Light Brigade 1854

LORD RAGLAN SAT ON TOP OF THE HILL
I SAY YOU CHAPS! THE HEAVY BRIGADE ARE BEATING THE RUSSIANS!
BOOM FIGHT FIGHT BANG

IT WAS TRUE
TELL LUCAN TO SEND THE LIGHT BRIGADE AFTER THEM!

SO RAGLAN SENT A MESSAGE TO LORD LUCAN...
Cavalry advance – You will be supported by foot soldiers
Raglan

'Forward the Light Brigade'

Was there a man dismayed?

LUCAN WAS PUZZLED
I'M PUZZLED. WHAT DO I ATTACK? AND DOES HE WANT ME TO WAIT FOR THE FOOT SOLDIERS TO ARRIVE?

SO LUCAN DID NOTHING. THE RUSSIANS RECOVERED AND STARTED PINCHING THE BRITISH CANNON
THEY'RE PINCHING OUR CANNON! WHAT'S LUCAN DOING? NOTHING!
BANG

Someone had blundered.

HE CALLED CAPTAIN NOLAN TAKE THIS MESSAGE TO LUCAN NOW!	*Theirs not to make reply*
Theirs not to reason why	 **THE SECOND MESSAGE READ..** Attack immediately Stop the enemy carrying away the guns *Raglan*
  **CAPTAIN NOLAN TOOK THE MESSAGE LUCAN WAS EVEN MORE PUZZLED...** WHICH GUNS?	*Theirs but to do and die*
Into the valley of Death	 LUCAN WASN'T AS HIGH UP AS LORD RAGLAN HE COULDN'T SEE THEM TAKING BRITISH GUNS. THE ONLY GUNS HE COULD SEE WERE THE RUSSIAN GUNS POINTED STRAIGHT DOWN THE VALLEY. IT WOULD BE SUICIDE. ORDERS ARE ORDERS - ATTACK! FOLLOW ME! WHY ME

> LUCAN SENT CARDIGAN, AND THE LIGHT BRIGADE ATTACKED THE WRONG GUNS
>
> CHARGE!

Rode the six hundred.

> NOLAN WAS FIRST TO BE KILLED – HIS CHEST RIPPED OPEN BY SHELL SPLINTERS
>
> OUGH!

Cannon to right of them,
Cannon to left of them,
Cannon in front of them
Volleyed and thundered;

> HORSES AGAINST GUNS – IT WAS NO CONTEST. THE LIGHT BRIGADE ATTACKED BRAVELY – AND MOST OF THE 600 DIED

Stormed at with shot and shell
While horse and hero fell,
They that had fought so well
Came through the jaws
*   of Death*
Back from the mouth of hell,

Tennyson finished with the words ...
When can their glory fade?
Oh, the wild charge they made!
All the world wondered.
Honour the charge they made,
Honour the Light Brigade,
Noble six hundred!
A Frenchman who watched the charge from high on a ridge had a different point of view. General Bosquet muttered the famous words ...
It's magnificent, but it isn't war – it's stupidity!

Vile Victorian soldering – or, Let's have a whip round for the soldiers

Would you have liked to fight in the Victorian army? Smart red uniforms (made you a good target for the enemy!). Officers who lived like gentlemen and treated the men like servants.

> RIGHT SMITH, AFTER YOU'VE POLISHED MY BOOTS, ATTACK THAT ARMY OVER THERE, AND IF YOU'RE NOT BACK IN TIME TO SERVE ME MY TEA I'LL HAVE YOU FLOGGED

And if the enemy didn't get you then your own army might! Apart from being killed by the enemy you could end up...

Flogged to death

Private Slim died after being punished by 50 lashes in 1867. He was lucky! In 1846 Private White died after receiving 150 lashes. In 1825 a soldier was sentenced to 1900 lashes – they stopped after he'd received 1200 and he survived. Maybe their arms got tired.

Frozen to death
At Balaclava in 1854 soldiers found something to help them survive the cold. Chocolate. But they didn't eat it!

Chocolate used to be sent out to us, this reaching us made up in shape like a big flat cheese; this chocolate we found would burn so, breaking it into pieces and piling stones around we would set fire to it, this being the only way we succeeded in staying warm for the first few months.

WHAT SHALL WE HAVE FOR SUPPER?

HOW ABOUT A CUP OF HOT CHOCOLATE?

Murdered
A sergeant had a soldier put in prison for gambling. He then had the man released... but the soldier wasn't going to forgive.

Loading his musket, he watched for the return of the sergeant and shot him through the back as he was about to enter his room.

Executed
Striking an officer could be punished by death.

One man struck the doctor while in hospital. He was shot. I saw this. It was early in the morning. Everything was so still that a pin might be heard to fall. The coffin was put on the ground. The man knelt upon his own coffin. The crack of the muskets was heard and the man fell dead.

Dying of thirst

Many soldiers died from lack of water in droughts in India. One sad case was of a soldier who helped to save the town of Lucknow. He received a deadly wound and lay dying. Some English ladies had been living in Lucknow at the time. The heat was terrible and the soldier was too ill to reach water. As the English ladies passed him, he begged the women to bring him a drop of water. They pointed to the well and said . . .

'THERE IS THE WELL, MY MAN, AND YOU CAN GET THE WATER YOURSELF'

He died.

Dying of hunger

When the enemy cut off supplies (in a siege) the soldiers could starve to death. In the Boer War in South Africa, the soldiers managed to joke about their pitifully small meals. They said grace after a meal –
We thank the Lord for what we've had,
If it were more we should have been glad.
But as the times are rather bad,
We've got to be glad with what we've had.

And after all that . . .
If a soldier survived he retired.
The grateful Victorian government paid him a pension of less than 4p a day.

Vile Victorian villians

The Victorian villains were as vile as any you'd never wish to meet. The real villains would cut your throat, poison you, club you to death or shoot you just for the sake of your purse.

As if these thieves and murderers weren't bad enough in real life the Victorians made up even worse horrors in their books. Count Dracula, Frankenstein's Monster and Doctor Jekyll and Mr Hyde were all Victorian inventions.

The viler the crimes the viler the punishments. The Victorians liked nothing better than a good hanging to bring out the crowds. All in all it was a vile and violent time to live.

The real live vile Victorian villains

Jack The Ripper

For over a hundred years police, historians, writers and criminal experts have tried to work out who the dreaded 'Jack the Ripper' could have been. He was never caught. Why did he kill? Why did he stop?

Many books have been written by people who claim they can 'prove' who the killer is. But each new book proves the other writers are wrong. The writers have claimed that Jack the Ripper was the following. Which one would you choose?

A mad London doctor called Stanley
A mad Russian doctor called Pedachenko
An unnamed butcher
A lawyer called Druitt
Queen Victoria's grandson, the Duke of Clarence (Her Majesty always showed an unusual interest in the case!)

The Duke of Clarence's best friend, James Stephen (who was hit on the head by the sail of a windmill and became mad)
The Duke of Clarence's doctor, William Gull
An artist named Sickert
A bootmaker called Kaminsky
A believer in black magic called D'Onston.
Or would you go for one of the wilder ideas? Someone at some time has said it was . . .
A policeman (perhaps a senior policeman destroyed important evidence – to protect one of his officers?)
A man dressed as a woman
A cannibal
A Canadian wearing snow shoes
A woman – Jill the Ripper?
The truth is that nobody really knows who Jack the Ripper was. He (or she) killed just eight women but became a legend as the vilest Victorian of all.

If you ever find out the killer's true identity, and if you can prove it, you could sell your story for a million pounds.

Mary Ann Cotton

If the vilest criminal is the one who murders the most then Britain's worst killer of all time killed four times as many victims as Jack the Ripper. Men, women, children and little babies. And it isn't a man ... it's a woman.

She lived in the North Eastern corner of England and not many people have heard of her. In July 1872, in West Auckland, County Durham, an inquest was held into the death of a little boy, Charles Edward Cotton. The jury had to listen to the evidence and decide how he died. Was it ...

'Natural Causes' – he died of an illness?

'Murder' – did someone kill him deliberately? And how?

'Manslaughter' – did someone kill him accidentally?

'Suicide' – did Charles Edward kill himself?

Here is the evidence. What do you think the jury decided?

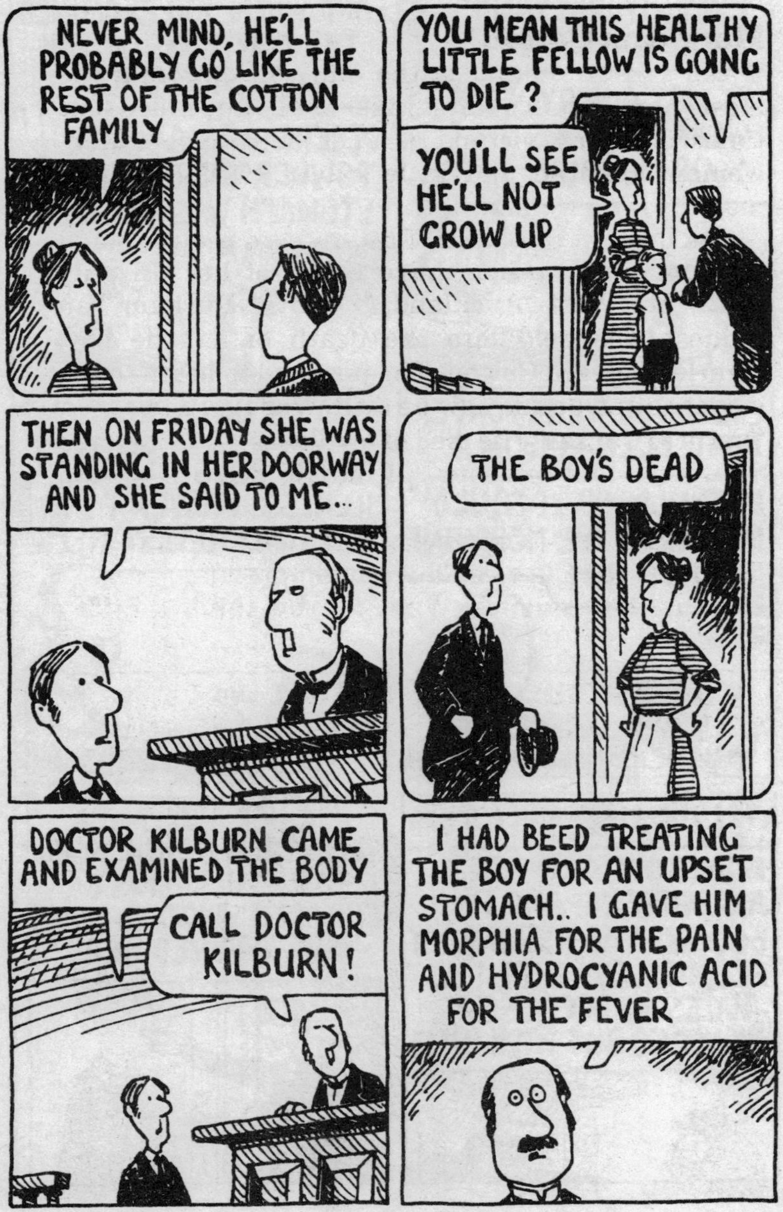
NEVER MIND, HE'LL PROBABLY GO LIKE THE REST OF THE COTTON FAMILY
YOU MEAN THIS HEALTHY LITTLE FELLOW IS GOING TO DIE ?
YOU'LL SEE HE'LL NOT GROW UP
THEN ON FRIDAY SHE WAS STANDING IN HER DOORWAY AND SHE SAID TO ME...
THE BOY'S DEAD
DOCTOR KILBURN CAME AND EXAMINED THE BODY
CALL DOCTOR KILBURN !
I HAD BEED TREATING THE BOY FOR AN UPSET STOMACH.. I GAVE HIM MORPHIA FOR THE PAIN AND HYDROCYANIC ACID FOR THE FEVER

ISN'T HYDROCYANIC ACID A POISON ?
IT WAS A VERY WEAK MIXTURE YOUR HONOUR
AND WHEN YOU EXAMINED THE CONTENTS OF THE BOY'S STOMACH?
THERE WAS A WHITE POWDER THERE - THE STOMACH WAS INFLAMED
COULD THE WHITE POWDER HAVE BEEN POISON ?
IT COULD - OR IT COULD HAVE BEEN THE MORPHINE I GAVE HIM
AND THE INFLAMMATION? POISON ?
OR THE BOY'S ILLNESS. I HAVEN'T HAD TIME TO TEST IT
CALL MRS MARY ANN COTTON
I GAVE MY STEP-SON ARROWROOT - AND I BOUGHT THE ARROWROOT FROM RILEY THERE ! HE HATES ME BECAUSE I WON'T GO OUT WITH HIM!
ASK HER ABOUT HER HUSBAND'S DEATH, AND HER OTHER THREE CHILDREN WHO DIED SINCE SHE ARRIVED HERE!

> SILENCE IN COURT! THE JURY MUST FORGET THEY EVER HEARD THAT REMARK. NOW, JURY, YOU DECIDE. DID CHARLES EDWARD DIE OF POISONING? IF SO, WHO POISONED HIM AND WAS IT DELIBERATE OR ACCIDENTAL? OR DID CHARLES EDWARD DIE NATURALLY OF A STOMACH FEVER?

If you were the jury what would you have decided?
Verdict: The West Auckland jury decided that Charles Edward died naturally of a stomach fever! Mary Ann Cotton was free.

Then the local newspapers checked her past life and found she had moved around the North of England and lost three husbands, a lover, a friend, her mother and at least a dozen children! And they had all died of stomach fevers!

Doctor Kilburn then tested the white powder in Charles Edward's stomach. It was the deadly poison, arsenic. Mary Ann Cotton was tried for murder, found guilty and hanged at Durham Jail in 1873.

The vile Victorian children made up a nasty little skipping song about her. It was sung in the streets of Durham till quite recently. It went:

> *Mary Ann Cotton*
> *She's dead and she's rotten*
> *She lies in her bed*
> *With her eyes wide open.*
> *Sing, sing, oh what can I sing?*
> *Mary Ann Cotton is tied up with string.*
> *Where? Where? Up in the air*
> *Selling black puddings a penny a pair.*

Mary Ann Cotton got away with killing at least 15 and maybe as many as 20 people because . . .

1 Poison was easy to buy. Arsenic mixed with soap was sold in chemists' shops as a killer of bed-bugs. Wash away the soap and you would be left with pure arsenic.

2 Arsenic poisoning gave the victim sickness and diarrhoea – so did gastric (or stomach) fever. Busy doctors couldn't tell the difference.

3 A cheap baby food was flour mixed with water. Mothers fed this to babies and didn't realise that it gave their babies stomach upsets. Sickness in babies was very common. A doctor would see a sick baby and not think it unusual or suspicious.

4 Death was very common in the Victorian times. In the 1880s a quarter of all people died in their first year, a half were dead by the time they were 20 and three quarters were dead by 40. Mary Ann was thought to be 'unlucky' to lose so many during her stay in West Auckland, but nobody (except Riley) thought it was unbelievable.

5 Mary Ann Cotton moved about the North East. Each time she remarried she changed her name. Nobody could know the trail of deaths she left in her wake because nobody made the connection between Mrs Robson, Mrs Ward, Mrs Robinson and Mrs Cotton, who had all lost husbands and children in different towns.

Don't worry! Police experts reckon she would not get away with it today!

The vile Victorian make-believe villains

As if Jack the Ripper and Mary Ann Cotton weren't enough for the Victorians to read about in their newspapers, they wanted to read about violent crime in their books and magazines. Popular, cheap crime papers were called *Penny Dreadfuls*. New and horrific criminals were invented to satisfy the readers. Even today there are many people who believe these villains really existed. Villains like . . .

Sweeney Todd – the Demon Barber of Fleet Street

The sailor rubbed his bristling chin. He needed a shave. He looked along Fleet Street for the familiar sign of a barber's shop: a red-and-white striped pole. He soon spotted one over the door of number 186. The name plate said, *Sweeney Todd – Barber*.

The sailor pushed open the door and entered the dim and musty room that smelled of soap. A large, red-faced man watched him from the shadows. 'Good morning, sir! A nice close shave, perhaps?'

'Ah, yes!' the customer said and squinted through the gloom. The chair in the middle of the room was dark and heavy and hard. He sat in it wearily.

'I'll just bolt the door, sir,' the barber said. 'I'll polish you off then close for lunch.'

The sailor heard the heavy bolts slide into the door with a booming that rang through the room. 'There. We won't be disturbed!'

The barber picked up a bowl and a brush and whipped up a rich, thick lather. He began to talk while the sailor closed his eyes and lay back. 'Yes, nearly time for lunch. Have you had lunch yet? No? Ah, I'm the luckiest man in London, there. I live next to the best pie shop in the city. Mrs Lovatt's meat pies are famous. People come from miles to buy them.'

The sailor grunted and Sweeney Todd the barber brushed the foaming soap gently into his bristling beard.

'You've never heard of Mrs Lovatt's pies? You do surprise me! You must be a stranger? Yes? You don't know London then? No? And no one in London knows you, I suppose.'

The only sound in the room was the soft sizzle of the soap bubbles settling. The barber took a razor from the bench and slowly sharpened it on a leather strap that hung beside the mirror. He looked at his own face in the mirror and grinned. 'It's sad to be alone in a big city, sir. No one to talk to. And no one to miss you if you disappeared . . .'

Sweeney Todd walked towards the sailor with the razor catching a chink of light that had crept through the dust-crusted windows. He brought the razor closer to the customer's trusting face. 'We'll have you finished in no time, sir!' the barber chuckled.

Something in his voice made the sailor open his eyes. He looked up into the shiny face of the barber and the razor-bright eyes. He opened his mouth to cry out.

Sweeney Todd pressed a small metal catch with his foot and the chair rocked backwards. The floor opened and the chair disappeared into a black hole. There was a cry of terror, a crunch as the sailor's head hit the stone cellar floor below. Then a sudden silence.

The barber put his razor down carefully. He pulled at a rope and the chair rose back into its place – empty now. A click of the catch and it was ready for the next customer . . . or victim.

Sweeney Todd wiped his sweating hands on his greasy apron and walked towards a door at the back of his shop. The door led to stone steps down into the cellar.

The Demon Barber of Fleet Street looked at the broken body of his latest prey and nodded happily. He crossed the floor of the cellar and came to the steps that led upwards into the shop next door. He tapped on the door and tugged it open a touch.

The warm smell of fresh-baked pies met his nostrils. 'Ah, Mrs Lovatt,' he said gently, 'One of your delicious meat pies, if you please.'

The smiling woman handed him a steaming plate and looked at him with one eyebrow raised, questioning.

Todd nodded. 'Yes, Mrs Lovatt. You'll find a nice, fresh supply of meat on the cellar floor ....'

Of course, Sweeney Todd never really existed, but a hundred years later his story is still told and has even been made into a musical play!

Ask ten sensible adults about Sweeney Todd – or ten teachers if you can't find any sensible adults. See how many think it may be a true story. But it isn't! It really isn't!

The real dead vile Victorian villains

Public executions

If the real villains of Victorian Britain were caught then they faced fearsome punishments. They could be sent to the 'hulks' – ancient ships tied up by the river. By day the villains would break stones, clear sewers or move earth for building works. By night they would return in iron chains to the filthy, crowded ships where disease killed many. In 1841, at the start of Victoria's reign, there were 3625 prisoners in these floating prisons on the Thames. By 1857 there were none. (The villains had been transported to Australia.)

But they still faced the death penalty by hanging. And hanging in public.

Foul facts about public executions

In 1846 public executions were held outside Newgate Prison. Rich people paid between 20 and 50 guineas (a guinea was a bit more than a pound) to rent the houses opposite the prison to have a good view of seven pirates being executed. (That's several thousand pounds in today's values!)

Charles Dickens said . . .

I believe public execution to be a savage horror behind the time.

But he wasn't against executions going on inside the prison walls.

In 1856 a group of politicians from the House of Commons said that public executions should end. The House of Lords rejected the idea. They said that executing someone in public set an example to other people who thought about committing a crime.

The Lords' decision was popular with many people who did good business at executions ... for example, the sellers of 'ballads' – popular poems written about the murderer. The poetry was usually awful.

Franz Muller was executed for the murder of an old man in a railway carriage in 1864 – the first ever railway murder. He tried to escape to America but was brought back to face a trial. He confessed to the murder in the final second before the gallows trap-door opened and he fell to his death. The poems written about him were crimes against the art of poetry! They included terrible lines like ...

> *That fatal night I was determined*
> *Poor Thomas Briggs to rob and slay*
> *And in the fatal railway carriage,*
> *That night, I took his life away.*
> *His crimson gore did stain the carriage.*
> *I threw him from the train, alack!*
> *I, on the railway, left him bleeding.*
> *I robbed him of his watch and hat.*

About 50,000 people attended Muller's execution. The day after, *The Times* newspaper reported ...
None will ever believe the open manner in which garrotting and highway robbery were carried on.
In 1868, public hangings were stopped – not because they were inhuman, but because they caused so much crime and death among the crowds that went to see them!

The man they could not hang

Not everyone was as successfully executed as Franz Muller. Twenty years after Muller's crime, a middle-aged man, John Lee, had been working for a Miss Emma Keyse who had once been a maid to Queen Victoria. After an argument she cut his wages – in return he cut her throat.

He was tried and sentenced to hang. The hangman's name was Berry. Mr Berry placed a hood over Lee's head, put the rope round his neck, then pulled the lever to open the trapdoor. Nothing happened!

Berry jumped up and down on the trapdoor. Still nothing happened. Lee was taken back to his cell to wait while the machinery was tested. It worked perfectly. Lee was brought back.

Mr Berry placed a hood over Lee's head, put the rope round his neck then pulled the lever to open the trapdoor again. Nothing happened! Again Berry tested it. Again it worked perfectly.

Third time lucky perhaps? Mr Berry placed a hood over Lee's head once more, put the rope round his neck, then pulled the lever to open the trapdoor. Nothing happened!

It was thought that wet weather had swelled the wood and Lee's weight made the trapdoor jam shut.

The local justice ordered a postponement of the execution until the government minister had been informed of the strange events. At last the reply came . . .

Don't try again. John Lee is to be imprisoned for life instead.

John Lee's neck got away with murder!

Five further facts about John Lee:
1 Lee served 22 years in prison and then was released.
2 No one knows what happened to him after he was released.
3 Some people thought he was innocent of the crime. The sticking trapdoor was God's way of making sure that justice was done.
4 A film was made about the case and called, *The Man They Could Not Hang*.
5 A pop group has called itself, *The Men They Couldn't Hang*.

Criminals

Victorians thought they could tell a criminal by his looks and general appearance! Things they looked for were:

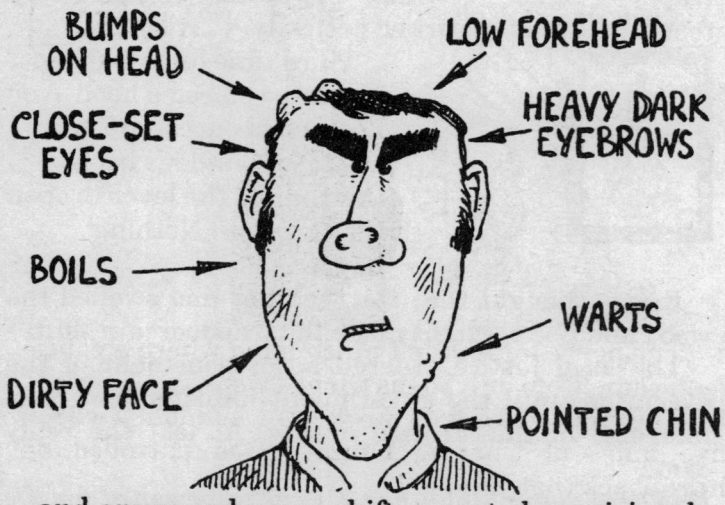

- BUMPS ON HEAD
- LOW FOREHEAD
- CLOSE-SET EYES
- HEAVY DARK EYEBROWS
- BOILS
- WARTS
- DIRTY FACE
- POINTED CHIN

... and anyone who was shifty or acted suspiciously. Most of the population were like this really!

The Victorian police ... or, Has anything changed?

Sir Robert Peel had invented the police in London in 1829 to try and prevent the sort of crime the Victorians suffered. Perhaps they did some good but ...

1 Early policemen were paid just one shilling (5p) a day. A shilling was called a 'bob' and policemen were called 'bobbies' (Bobby is also the nickname of someone called Robert – so they could have taken their name from Sir 'Robert' Peel).

2 Really clever people would be earning much more than a shilling at other jobs – so the police force didn't attract many really clever bobbies.

3 The police force employed practically anyone – even if the man could barely read or write.

4 The police force didn't much mind where a policeman came from or who his friends were.

5 The first police only worked in London – within five miles of Charing Cross – and patrolled on **horse**back (not pandas)!

6 It wasn't until 1856 that the rest of the country had paid policemen.

Epilogue

The Victorian age wasn't all vile, of course.

The Victorians were energetic and inventive. By the time the old Queen died we had electric lights . . . and electric chairs.

We had motor cars . . . and crashes.

We had schools . . . and teachers.

We had the very, very rich . . . and the very, very poor.

Every silver lining has a cloud, as they say.

Charles Dickens wrote brilliant novels . . . and he wrote some pretty vile stuff.

But, when he was writing well he was one of the best. He wrote a brilliant summary of France in the 1790s, after the French Revolution. He could have been writing about the Victorian age. It sums it all up pretty well.

It was the best of times, it was the worst of times, it was the age of wisdom, it was the age of foolishness, it was the season of Light, it was the season of Darkness, it was the spring of hope, it was the winter of despair, we had everything before us, we had nothing before us, we were going direct to Heaven, we were all going direct the other way.
A Tale of Two Cities

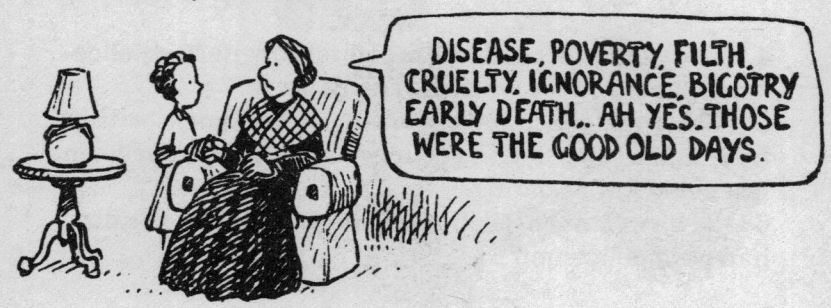

> DISEASE, POVERTY, FILTH, CRUELTY, IGNORANCE, BIGOTRY, EARLY DEATH... AH YES. THOSE WERE THE GOOD OLD DAYS.

VILE VICTORIANS

GRISLY QUIZ

Now find out if you're a vile Victorian expert!

Howzat Victoria?

The English lost a cricket match against Australia for the first time in 1880. They burned a bail to ashes and have played for those Ashes ever since. 'How's that?' the cricketers cried (or 'Howzat?' in cricket language) when they thought a batsman was out. And 'Howzat?' is the question about these curious Queen Victoria facts.

1. She was the shortest and the longest reigning monarch Britain ever had! Howzat?
2. Victoria was responsible for the death of her beloved husband, Albert. Howzat?
3. The police set Victoria up as the target for a murdering gunman. Howzat?
4. Victoria was highly respectable all her life yet she caused a scandal in her coffin. Howzat?
5. Albert and Victoria were married in 1840 though he never proposed to her. Howzat?
6. The Victorians liked portrait paintings but she preferred a particular kind. Howzat?
7. Victoria was Queen of England yet the 'Queen's English' was never very good. Howzat?

Manchester Misery

Not many men in Victorian England were gentlemen – which was unfortunate because gentlemen lived longer than working men. If you were an upper class person living in Manchester in 1842 you could expect to live 38 years (on average). But, if you were in the working class what was the average you could expect to live?
a) 37 years b) 27 years c) 17 years

Umms and Errs

The 1800s were the age of the melodrama. Before the days of television the century's soap operas took place in thrilling theatres where villainous Victorians battled against hapless heroes. You just know what they are going to say ... or do you?

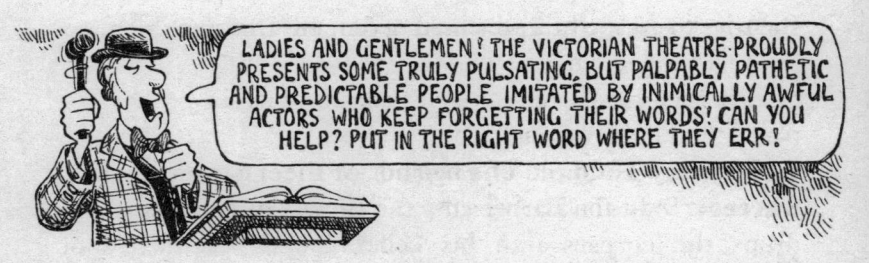

1. East Lynne

Poor Isabel leaves her husband but sneaks back (disguised as a governess) to nurse her sickly son. He dies in her arms as Isabel cries...

Oh, Willie, my child! Dead! Dead! Dead! And never called me **errrr!**

2. Youth
A bunch of English soldiers struggle against the enemy who must be evil because they aren't English. (The Victorians could be nasty racists.) Their colonel encourages them...

Remember, Great England is looking at you! Show how her sons can fight and **errr**!

3. The Fatal Marriage
Poor Isabella loses her husband and marries a dear friend. Then her first husband returns. She tries to murder him then decides to stab herself instead. (Don't try this at home.) Isabella sobs...

When I am dead, forgive me and **errr** *me!*

4. The Harp of Altenberg
Our heroine, Innogen, is captured by the villain, Brenno. As she tries to escape he grabs hold of her and Innogen cries...

Errrr *me!*

5. Sweeney Todd or, The Barber of Fleet Street
Sweeney Todd the Barber cuts the throats of customers and drops the corpses into his cellar. There his next-door neighbour collects the bodies and chops them up to make meat pies. As Sweeney cuts a throat he cries...

I **errrr** *them off!*

6. Maria Marten or, Murder in the Red Barn
Based on a true 1827 murder. William Corder waits in the barn

for sweet Maria but plans to shoot her. Corder sneers...

I now await my victim. Will she come? Yes, for women are foolish enough to do anything for the men they **errrr!**

QUICK QUESTIONS

1. How old were the youngest chimney sweeps in 1804? (Clue: not infants)

2. How was Lord Nelson's body brought home after his death at Trafalgar in 1805? (Clue: not a barrel of laughs)

3. John Bellingham blamed the government for ruining his business. How did he get his revenge in 1812? (Clue: a blow to the head)

4. Napoleon lost the Battle of Waterloo in 1815. What did Brit General Lord Raglan lose? (Clue: 'armless sort of chap)

5. In 1817 Brixton prison invented a new punishment for criminals. What? (Clue: hamster toy)

6. In 1818 Mary Shelley wrote a horrific story that is still popular today. What is it called? (Clue: frankly monstrous)

7. In 1820 in Scotland a rebel weaver was the last man to be sentenced to an ancient punishment. What? (Clue: long and drawn out)

8. In 1821 Queen Caroline died. What did this odd queen put on her head to keep cool while she was out riding? (Clue: American pie)

9. In 1822 King George IV visited Scotland and wore a kilt. How did he keep his knees warm? (Clue: they weren't loose)

10. In 1823 a boy at a public school, William Webb Ellis, cheated at football and invented a new game. What? (Clue: you have to hand it to him)

11. In Edinburgh in 1828 WilliamBlake was accused of 16 murders. What did he do with the bodies? (Clue: they were a little cut up about it)

Answers

Howzat Victoria?
1) She was the shortest in height but the longest in the time she spent on the throne.
2) The dirty water from her toilet leaked into Albert's drinking water and gave him the disease that killed him.
3) The gunman tried to shoot her as she drove in her carriage in London. His gun misfired and he escaped. The police told her to drive in the same place and at the same time the next day so that he could try again. He did! They caught him.
4) She was buried with a photograph of her 'friend', her Scottish servant. In her hand was a lock of his hair. What had they been up to when she was alive, people wanted to know!
5) Victoria proposed to him!
6) Victoria (and hubby Albert) preferred the people in the pictures to have no clothes on!
7) She was from the German Hanover family so she always spoke with a German accent.

Manchester Misery
c) In London slums people would, on average, live 22 years – but average upper class people would live twice as long. The unhealthiest place to live in 1842 was Liverpool, where the average age of death was just 15 years old. Queen Victoria lived to be 81. The average age was so low because lots of children died very young.

Umms and Errs
1) **Mother**. 'On the telephone' is definitely wrong! So is 'a taxi'.
2) **Die**. 'Fight and win' would not be very English – look at the present-day cricket team.
3) **Pity**. 'Bury' makes a bit more sense, you have to admit.
4) **Unhand**. Not a word you'll hear very often but remember it next time a history teacher grabs you!
5) **Polish**. This is such a famous line your granny probably knows it. In fact she probably ate the pies!
6) **Love**. 'Get chocolates from' is not a good enough answer.

Quick Questions
1) Four years old. The sweeps weren't supposed to be under nine but employers lied about the ages of their workers.
2) Pickled in a barrel of brandy. It preserved the body – and the sailors drank the brandy afterwards!
3) He shot the Prime Minister, Spencer Perceval, dead. The only Brit PM to be assassinated. Bellingham was hanged.
4) His arm. He also almost lost his wedding ring when the arm was amputated. 'Here! Bring that arm back!' he cried

from his hospital bed.

5) The 'treadmill' – a bit like a hamster wheel, where the prisoners walk and walk and go nowhere.

6) Frankenstein. Monstrous Mary was only 18 when she dreamed up this story of a man put together like a Lego kit. Seriously weird writer.

7) Wilson was sentenced to be hanged, drawn and quartered. In fact he was hanged then beheaded. His 'crime' was to lead a march in protest against unemployment.

8) A pumpkin. She probably changed it each time she rode, which is more than she did with her stockings. She wore them till they stank.

9) Tights. He had them made the colour of his flesh because he didn't want to look like a wimp.

10) Rugby. He picked up the ball and ran with it. The game was named after his public school, Rugby, so we don't say, 'Fancy a game of Ellis?'

11) He sold them to doctors so they could experiment on them. Of course the doctors weren't punished.

INTERESTING INDEX

Where will you find 'bottom-slapping',
'fried earwigs' and 'mice on toast' in an index?
In a Horrible Histories book, of course!

Afghan Wars 101
Albert, Prince (Queen Victoria's husband) 8-9, 12-15
American Civil War 102
amputations 105
army 99-111
arsenic (poison) 118
Ashes (cricket disaster) 9

baby-farmers 23-4
Balaclava, battle of 105, 110
Barnardo, Doctor (opened homes for orphans) 25-7
Bartholomew Fair 10
bears 60
bed-bugs 118
Beeton, Mrs (cook) 92
bishopophobia (fear of bishops) 16
black magic 113
Blackburn Rovers FC 61
bluebottles, stewed 90-1
Blumenfeld, R.D. (writer) 79
body-finders 77
Boer Wars 100-1, 111

books, serious 70-1
Boot, Mr (chemist) 8
bottom-slapping 60
boxing 58
brains, overheating 97
Brown, John (Victoria's manservant) 14, 20
Buckland, Frank (naturalist and son of William) 90
Buckland, William (doctor) 90
Burnley FC 61
Byron, George (poet) 100

caning 45, 47
cannibals 113
Cardigan, Lord (soldier in charge of the Light Brigade) 105, 108
cavalry (soldiers on horses) 105
cesspools 78
chimney sweeps 43
chocolate 100, 110
cholera 6, 10, 76
Christian, Prince (Victoria's son-in-law) 20
Clarence, Duke of (Victoria's grandson) 112-13
Cocking, Robert (balloonist) 10

Collins, Wilkie (novelist) 7
corn laws 74
Cotton, Mary Ann (murderer) 114-19
crime
    prevention 127
    punishment 44-7, 112, 123-4
Crimean War 9, 94, 99, 104

Darling, Grace (sea-rescuer) 7
death
    rates 85
    by flogging 109-11
    by hunger 111
    by ribbons 43
    in surgery 7
Dickens, Charles (novelist) 9, 48, 70, 77, 123, 128
disinfectants 7
Disraeli, Benjamin (prime minister) 14
doctors 23, 51, 87
dogs 56-7, 59
Dracula, Count (fictional villain) 112

earwigs, fried 91
Edward (duke of Kent) 12
Edward VII (king of England) 21
elephants 21, 90, 102

factories, rules 51, 81-5
famine 8
flogging (whipping) 99, 109
food, foul 90-3
Francis, John (gunman) 15
Frankenstein's Monster (fictional villain) 112
freezing to death 85, 110
French Revolution 128
funerals 86-7

gallows 124
Galton, Francis (scientist) 97-8
games, gruesome 54-63
garrotting 124
George III (king of England) 12
Gilbert, W.S. (composer) 94-5
Gladstone, William (prime minister) 14
glass eyes 20
Gordon, Adam L. (poet) 99
Graham, Harry (poet) 72
grave diggers 86
Great Exhibition 7
Greenwood, James (writer) 24
gunpowder, drinking 97

hags 18
hangings 24, 117
    crowds at 112
    public 123-4
    unsuccessful 125-6
highway robbery 124
Holmes, Sherlock (fictional detective) 8
Hood, Thomas (poet) 81
Humphrey, James (soldier) 100

Indian Mutiny 10, 100-2
industrial revolution 73
inspectors 53, 77

Jack the Ripper (murderer) 11, 112-14, 119
Jekyll, Dr/Hyde, Mr (fictional villain) 112

Khalid, Said (Zanzibar rebel) 103

laws
    child mine workers 7, 40
    corn 74
Lee, John (murderer) 125-6

leeches 21
lice 104
Light Brigade, Charge of 99, 105-8
Lister, Joseph (surgeon) 7
Lucan, Lord (cavalry commander) 105-8

Majuba Hill, battle of 101
Martineau, Harriet (writer) 17-18
Melbourne, Lord (doctor) 19
Meyers, Doctor (inventor of tapeworm "cure") 87
mice on toast 90
mines, children in 7, 32-40, 42
monkeys, as dinner guests 60
mould runners (child pottery workers) 83
Muller, Franz (murderer) 124

nails, hammered through ears 42
Napoleonic Wars 99
Night Soil Men (toilet contents collectors) 55
Nightingale, Florence (nurse) 9, 94, 104
Nolan, Captain (soldier) 107-8

The Old Curiosity Shop (Novel by Charles Dickens) 70-1
orphans 25

paupers 86-7
Peel, Robert (founder of police) 94, 127
Penny Black (stamp) 7
Penny Dreadfuls (crime newspapers) 119
Pilcher, Percy (hang-glider) 11
pillories 51
pirates 123
plays 66-9
Pratt, William W. (playwright) 66

Raglan, Lord (army commander) 99, 106-7

railways 78, 80
 murder on 124
 underground 79
rats 56-7
ratting (sport) 56-7
Rawson, Rear Admiral (naval commander) 103
Rothschild, Baron 60

Sanitary Commission 91
Schoenberg, Arnold (composer) 89
schools 9-10, 44-53, 128
seances 14
Sedgwick, John (American general) 102
servants, life of 25-32
sewers 57, 76-8, 123

Sheridan, Richard (playwright) 12
Simms, George (writer) 42
slums 85
snakes 60
soldiers, life of 109-11
speed limits 9
spiders, buttered 88
Spotsylvania, battle of 102
starvation 111
Stevenson, R.L. (novelist) 9
stocks 51
stomach upsets 118
superstitions, silly 88-9
sweatshops (clothing factories) 81

Talbot, William Henry Fox (photographer) 7
tapeworms 87
teachers 5-6, 12, 128
 screaming 51
 sensible 122
 terrible 44, 48-51
Tennyson, Alfred (poet laureate) 72, 105, 108

Thames, river
  prisons on 123
  sewage in 76-8
theatres 66
Todd, Sweeney (fictional barber/murderer) 119-22
toilets 7, 29-30, 55, 85, 104
Tottenham Hotspur FC 8, 101
trappers (child mine workers) 36

Unwashed, The Great 78

Victoria (queen of England) 7-8, 10, 12-21, 72, 76, 80, 95, 99-101, 112
villains 112-26

wages 27, 31, 35, 49, 74, 81, 125, 127
Walters, Margaret (baby-farmer) 23-4
wars 99-111
Webb, Matthew (swimmer) 11, 61
White, Private (soldier) 109
wigs 16
wildlife, massacred 97
William IV (king of England) 12
witches 89
Wordsworth, Dorothy (poet's sister) 96
Wordsworth, William (poet) 95
work 81-5
workhouses 114

zebra-drawn carriages 60
Zulus 11

Terry Deary was born at a very early age, so long ago he can't remember. But his mother, who was there at the time, says he was born in Sunderland, north-east England, in 1946 – so it's not true that he writes all *Horrible Histories* from memory. At school he was a horrible child only interested in playing football and giving teachers a hard time. His history lessons were so boring and so badly taught, that he learned to loathe the subject. *Horrible Histories* is his revenge.

Martin Brown was born in Melbourne, on the proper side of the world. Ever since he can remember he's been drawing. His dad used to bring back huge sheets of paper from work and Martin would fill them with doodles and little figures. Then, quite suddenly, with food and water, he grew up, moved to the UK and found work doing what he's always wanted to do: drawing doodles and little figures.

141

Make sure you've got the whole horrible lot!

HORRIBLE HISTORIES
AWESOME EGYPTIANS
TERRY DEARY & PETER HEPPLEWHITE
ILLUSTRATED BY MARTIN BROWN
ISBN: 978 0439 94403 8 £4.99

HORRIBLE HISTORIES
MEASLY MIDDLE AGES
TERRY DEARY ILLUSTRATED BY MARTIN BROWN
ISBN: 978 0439 94401 4 £4.99

HORRIBLE HISTORIES
ROTTEN ROMANS
TERRY DEARY ILLUSTRATED BY MARTIN BROWN
ISBN: 978 0439 94400 7 £4.99

HORRIBLE HISTORIES
WOEFUL SECOND WORLD WAR
Terry Deary, Illustrated by Martin Brown
ISBN: 978 0439 94399 4   £4.99

HORRIBLE HISTORIES
VICIOUS VIKINGS
Terry Deary, Illustrated by Martin Brown
ISBN: 978 0439 94405 2   £4.99

HORRIBLE HISTORIES
TERRIBLE TUDORS
Terry Deary & Neil Tonge, Illustrated by Martin Brown
ISBN: 978 0439 94406 9   £4.99

HORRIBLE HISTORIES
GROOVY GREEKS
Terry Deary, Illustrated by Martin Brown
ISBN: 978 0439 94402 1   £4.99

HORRIBLE HISTORIES HANDBOOKS

Pirates
IN BLOOD-CURDLING COLOUR!
Terry Deary Illustrated by Martin Brown
ISBN: 978 0439 95578 2 £5.99

Warriors
Terry Deary
ISBN: 978 0439 94330 7 £5.99

Knights
IN BLOOD-CURDLING COLOUR!
Terry Deary Illustrated by Martin Brown
ISBN: 978 0439 95577 5 £5.99

Don't miss these horribly handy handbooks for all the gore and more!